Teaching prereading skills

Christopher Walker
Senior Lecturer in Education and Reading Tutor
Mather College of Education

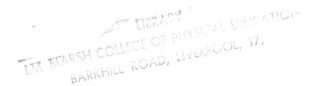
Ward Lock Educational

ISBN 0 7062 3423 5 paperback
    0 7062 3422 7 hardbound

First published 1975
Reprinted 1976

Set in 11 on 12 point Monotype Bembo
by Robert MacLehose and Company Limited
Printers to the University of Glasgow
for Ward Lock Educational
116 Baker Street, London W1M 2BB
Made in Great Britain

Contents

Introduction

Prereading comprises all the many activities used to develop the attitudes and skills that the child will need before the reading process can begin. Though teachers generally accept that early reading involves a much more complex set of processes than was formerly thought to be the case, in practice prereading is a much neglected field. In a great number of infant schools known to me personally reading readiness provision is minimal. In these schools the teachers most highly regarded as teachers of reading are those who are famed for getting the children away on books at the earliest possible moment, frequently during the first week at school. No attempt is made to pave the way first. Some children are obviously ready for such treatment and respond well. For those who have difficulty through such early confrontation with books, progress through the infant school is a constant war of attrition with the printed word. Some survive and read adequately, though with little pleasure. For many, the seeds of future reading failure or, at best, negative attitudes towards reading, are sown during the first months of schooling. If for many children learning to read is not fun, the actual teaching is sheer drudgery. Many teachers admittedly organize their day around the central need to hear each child reading individually as frequently as possible. When many of the children have been put on books too soon, their halting, stammering progress through the reading scheme unnecessarily lengthens the time spent on hearing reading, and such sessions become a dreary chore both for teacher and child. Time spent unproductively on hearing the unready also cuts down the time available for those who could profit from teacher inter-action and thus the potentially good readers are unnecessarily retarded. How to organize productively the vast proportion of the school day for all those children who at any one time are not working with the teacher is a constant nightmare. The result all too frequently is seen in those apparently interminable bouts of aimless drawing and colouring which occupy far too much of many an infant day. Now the purpose of pre-reading is to get all the children off to a good start in formal reading when they, at their different individual rates, are ready to accomplish this with confidence and success. When success attends the beginnings of reading, the teacher's task is a pleasant one, for she needs success as much as do her pupils.

Much greater attention to prereading in British schools is necessitated by the early age at which our children have traditionally started school. In most other advanced countries children do not start school until age six and in the Scandinavian countries they start at seven. If, in the United States and in Scandinavia, large numbers of children who are much more mature than ours have difficulty in beginning reading, a proportion of British children, because of their comparative developmental immaturity, can be expected to have even greater difficulty. With the very recent trend towards extending provision for nursery education we can expect our children to start school with even less linguistic and general developmental maturity than those we have been accustomed to introduce to reading.

The amount of prereading instruction that a given child requires depends upon a number of factors – emotional maturity and stability which affect confidence, effort and concentration; oral language facility which may be affected by home environment and social class; sensory and motor development which affect ability to discriminate both visually and aurally, and to coordinate hand and eye. Interest in books and motivation are also important. The child with a strong desire to read usually reads despite the difficulties involved. The child in whom the above factors seem highly developed may need little or no prereading instruction at all, and once he is socially settled in his new environment of school may make an early and successful start on reading. Others may be deficient in only one of the factors listed. Concentration on this one element may be all that is needed to get them off to a good start, and thus for such children the amount of prereading activity may be limited in range and of comparatively short duration. Others may be grossly deficient in a number of abilities and for them the range of prereading activities may be very extensive and of long duration.

Teachers vary in their ability to make accurate assessments of the different levels of readiness which groups and individuals in their classes exhibit. In the absence, as yet, of any suitable testing instruments, skilled observations of the indicators of readiness form the surest guides. Unfortunately teachers vary in their sensitivity and insight into children's needs. They vary also in the importance which they attach to reading. Some are better trained than others, some more experienced and some are more highly motivated towards self-improvement as teachers of reading. The latter more readily take and digest the literature on the teaching of reading, join the appropriate professional organizations such as the United Kingdom Reading Association, attend courses and gain extra qualifications in the subject. As teachers vary, so will the quality of their observations. They need to know what factors to observe and how to record them. They also need to know what to do to help the child when observations and records have been made. Not only do they need to know children's strengths and weaknesses, they also need to know a great deal about the nature of the early reading processes. Following Joyce Morris's famous dictum 'You can't teach what you don't know' it would be difficult to teach prereading if one had no idea of the nature of the processes for which prereading is the preparation. Consequently a considerable part of this book will be devoted to those aspects of child development the observation and recording of which are regarded as important for reading progress. Individual differences in child growth towards reading will be examined, especially those factors which appear to indicate reading failure. The skills of early reading competence will also be discussed at some length, for the major thesis of this book is that success in the skills of reading depends on successful acquisition of the related subskills of prereading. There will also be some discussion of materials, techniques and forms of organization appropriate for good prereading practice.

It is hoped that by giving rather more thorough and systematic attention to prereading than has formerly been the case, at the very least teachers will be able to identify sooner and more successfully those children who may be at risk as potential nonreaders, and not only identify them but give them appropriate treatment and training. Further, it is hoped that teachers may be better fitted to tailor experiences and activities to children so that when each child comes to reading he comes to it truly ready, and starts reading with such confidence, success and pleasure that positive attitudes to books and to reading are there when they count most – at the start.

Chapter 1

The importance of reading

Unless teachers are firmly convinced of the importance of reading in a modern society, they will not be motivated to teach reading well. Further, in a subject so crucial in its importance for success in school, for child growth and development, and for success in adult life, it is essential to make a good start. In a reading world the poor reader is often maladjusted; the illiterate frequently so. Very early in school the child who fails in reading is singled out from the majority of his peers by his inadequacy. The consequent loss of social prestige can lead either to withdrawal from normal school activity or to more aggressive antisocial behaviour by which he unconsciously seeks attention to his needs. Either reaction leads to rejection of school and its values and particularly to rejection of all learning associated with books. This is a pity, for the knowledge explosion of recent years has led to a considerable expansion of school curricula. Where once the three RS dominated the timetable a score of subjects now compete for time. Almost all the new subjects depend on the ability of children to read. Consequently almost all academic success is dependent on reading ability. So the child who cannot read becomes backward in almost everything else in school, and eleven years (the minimum period of compulsory schooling) is a long time to go on failing nearly all the time at nearly everything. Often the failing child turns to absenteeism but this gives only temporary relief. When he returns to school, unwillingly or no, he finds he has fallen more and more behind and his sense of failure is even more strongly reinforced.

On leaving school, the nonreader finds himself ill-prepared to face the demands of working life in a society where formal qualifications are highly prized. At a time when even the highly qualified face redundancy, what chance has the illiterate? Demand for unskilled labour is in rapid decline in the face of inexorable mechanization and automation. Socially, too, the nonreader has his problems. Accustomed to meeting the challenges of school by extremes of isolation or exhibitionism, he finds these reactions a poor preparation for adolescence when lasting friendships become important as personal relationships deepen and when friends of the opposite sex become desirable. Though the problems of the adult illiterate may appear to be somewhat remote from the small child starting school, the nursery/infant teacher must be constantly aware that many a man who cannot read was put off reading at the very beginning by being put on books too soon. Had the appropriate preliminaries been observed and the optimum moment seized many an illiterate might have been saved and much misery averted. Teachers of very young children have a fearsome responsibility for the happiness and well being of the society of tomorrow. It is indeed a pity that the society of today so inadequately prepares, supports and compensates them for the awesome responsibility with which it invests them.

Of much greater immediate concern to the nursery/infant teacher is the very considerable contribution that reading has to make to child growth and development. If we see our personalities as the sum total of our endowment and experience, a considerable part of that experience will have been acquired through the medium of print. How many of our ideas, fancies, theories, opinions and beliefs are truly of our own original devising? Most of us would have to admit, if pressed, that much of what we regard as our own thinking is largely the thinking of others, first seen in print, inwardly digested and finally adopted as our own. The more we can read the more we can extend our experience, range of interests and development of skills. The nonreader is dependent largely on the spoken word and direct experience which can only exist in the present. The competent reader knows no barriers of time and place; the whole of recorded knowledge and human experience is his for the taking. The nonreader's interests tend to be limited to the here, the now, the actual. Teachers of small children frequently encounter the 'butterfly' child whose interests lack depth and are so ephemeral that whatever stimuli are provided he is only attracted momentarily and cannot settle for more than a few seconds at anything. And yet, how wonderfully interest can widen and spiral, and new interests develop from former ones, especially if one can read. The development of children's interests is one of the major aims of teaching reading and one which is closely associated with what is to many one of education's principal goals, to arouse in the child a sense of wonder and curiosity in the world about him. Given a good start in reading he can begin to participate actively in exploring the world about him.

As the nonreader generally has few interests and limited means of developing them, so too the range of skills available to him is restricted and tends to be largely of a strictly practical kind. When he grows up it would be rare for an illiterate to be in any employment category other than unskilled because the skills that are prized by modern society are complex or highly specialized and generally require long courses of study, both in theory and practice, to reach acceptable levels of performance. The competent reader can make realistic appraisals of his abilities and by reading and study can develop his strengths to a high degree. He can also work on his weaknesses. Thus when the skills of the literate man are threatened by change he can adapt and apply them to new situations and enterprises. He can requalify himself by learning new skills. Children who make a bad start in reading have few avenues open to them when change threatens.

Many of us have envied the world of Don Quixote and his capacity to find adventure round every corner. For some favoured children for whom life provides a great wealth of stimulation there is variety enough to make growing up a challenging and exciting business. For many others in hospitals, institutions, the high flats of tower blocks and the downtown areas of our big cities, life is cribbed, cabinned and confined. In many of those urban areas which have been 'redeveloped' a grim uniformity prevails. For children in such environments it is difficult to squeeze adventure from such drab reality. To the small child on the fifteenth floor of a block of flats even playing with other children may be an infrequent luxury and when the child cannot read he can only turn inwards on himself or passively watch a succession of fleeting images flitting past him on the television screen. But for the reader adventures unlimited await him in the pages of literature. How easy it is for the child who can read to scale the walls of his modest home at will, to dive with Ralph and Peterkin in coral seas, to scale the Matterhorn with Whymper, to hide with Jim Hawkins in the apple barrel, to ask for more with Oliver Twist and travel far in time and space in the pages of Wells and Verne. Admittedly these experiences are vicarious, but one of the aims of teaching reading is to develop powers of imagination. In fact the reading of fiction or true adventure is hardly possible unless the reader brings some imagination to the task. The experiences which children gain from reading are second-hand, but small children lack the independence required to convert dream into reality. Once roused, however, the spirit of adventure is hard to dim. A great deal of reading was done to set Hilary's foot on Everest.

Not only does reading enable the child to share the adventures of others; it also enables him to acquire and share ideas. The child who can get ideas from books is interesting and often exciting to be with and thus he gains friendship and esteem. When faced with a problem the literate person can nearly always find a book which will help to resolve it, or he may meet in literature characters in similar or even more trying circumstances whose reactions are copied or considered and who thus bring comfort and relief. The reader has in books a means of exploring his own personality, of finding answers to the problems that beset him. The child who cannot read must find his own personality at times almost unfathomable.

When, by reading, we can increase our awareness of our own personalities and problems, we can the more easily begin to appreciate and understand the problems of others. By the evaluative processes involved in measuring up one set of problems against another we develop the beginnings of critical awareness and thinking. We reason and begin to use methods of logical inquiry. We sift the evidence and weigh it rather than rush to hasty, ill-considered conclusions. With the growth of reason comes toleration and understanding. The nonreading child is hindered in developing these qualities in that his only experience of problem-solving is limited to the concrete, personal and actual. He has difficulty in relating cause and effect, motive and consequence. Though the literate child may be prevented from acquiring first-hand personal experience due to his immaturity and lack of independence, he can build up over time a considerable number of 'case studies' from literature from which he can relate certain courses of action to their causes and likely effects. He can thus progressively grow in understanding of other people in a wide ranging way, not least by identification with, and by imitation of, the characters whom he has met in books. It is a short step from here to the discovery and illumination of ethical values. It is perhaps a fortunate feature of most early reading that characters are drawn sharply in either black or white. The author leaves his young readers in no doubt as to who is to be considered 'good' and which forms of behaviour 'bad'. The youngster who starts reading early soon acquires a battery of samples of behaviour which he can categorize as either morally bad or good. He need not depend entirely on his own personal experience of good or evil as often the nonreader must perforce do. As reading maturity grows the reader is enabled to acquire greater insights into ethical values by reading on planes much deeper than the obvious literal level of the test. The moral, psychological and philosophical undertones are unravelled from the surface level of the print by inference, implication and reasoning.

Mention has been made previously of the dull and restricting environments in which many youngsters have to grow up. In many a childhood there is little fun, little to excite one or look forward to and few escape routes from drabness, dullness and humourless uniformity. How fortunate is the child who can find fun from books when there is precious little of it in his real world. One of the pleasures of reading is that one can go on laughing about the same incident over and over again. I was reminded of the possibilities of reenjoyment available to the reader when I recently bought my youngest son, then twelve years old, a copy of *The Otterbury Incident*. He seemed to be a long time getting through it, over a week at least, which surprised me because he never seemed to have it out of his hand. When I asked him what the hold up was he astonished me by informing me that there was no hold up but that he was now reading it again for the fourteenth time in less than two weeks.

As well as giving opportunities for fun and escape, reading provides a safety valve for many a child who finds our modern culture over-regulated and confining. The middle-class child is generally considered to have numerous educational advantages which accrue to him from the cultural background by which his behaviour and attitudes are conditioned, though there can be little doubt that the acceptance of such a regime can often be extremely irksome. The misdeeds of the Nippers, Paddington and Charlie Brown provide a therapeutic outlet by which middle-class children can project their feelings of social nonconformity in socially approved ways – by reading. It might be pertinent to point out here that middle-class children are not universally advantaged from the point of view of reading readiness. They are frequently overprotected and overindulged, especially if they are only children, and when they are continually spoonfed throughout infancy are often not capable of the great personal effort required to begin to read. At the other extreme middle-class children have their share of parental neglect. Considerable numbers of middle-class mothers combine motherhood with full time jobs and professions. Aspiring executive fathers have notoriously heavy work schedules which leave them little time for their children, while the social mobility which particularly characterizes the middle classes as they move house for job promotion or social betterment can leave children in a constant state of emotional insecurity as they reluctantly forego former friendships and face the problem of breaking into new groups whose friendship patterns have already been formed.

What has been said so far has indicated that ability to read promotes normal mental health, child growth and development, and success in school and in adult life. What has been implied is that if reading is so important in a modern advanced society it is essential that the failure rate at the very beginning should be drastically reduced. However, not all observers agree that reading is as important as I have made it out to be and there are some who assert that people like myself, who admittedly have a vested interest in the teaching of reading, are accentuating its importance out of all proportion to its true significance in contemporary life and culture. The facts, however, prove that the reverse is true and that reading has been severely underrated in recent years. The Start and Wells enquiry of 1972 only served to highlight what educators on the shop floor had suspected for a number of years, namely that the gradual improvement of reading standards since the war had finally ground to a halt. The

Government was sufficiently concerned to commission the Bullock Committee to enquire into Reading and the Use of English in schools. Its brief is to consider how present practice may be improved, the role that initial and in-service training might play in contributing to improvement and to what extent arrangements for monitoring the general level of attainment in the skills of reading, writing and speech can be introduced or improved. To its credit the education service has not been content to await a government commission and whatever it may recommend, but has been engaging in self-help for some years past. In response to demands from the schools for better professional training, college of education initial courses in the teaching of reading have had much needed growth and extension. In-service courses in teaching reading in colleges of education, by the Open University, and in the rapidly growing teachers centres and reading centres have proliferated but still cannot satisfy the demands placed upon them. The plain fact is that the nation's teachers, who are employed by the state to transmit the society's culture, accord to literacy a central place both as part of the culture itself and as the principal agency of its transmission.

Many people engaged in education are concerned that print has such prominence in modern life. Most of us feel some regret that life cannot be lived more fully rather than merely read about. But we in these islands no longer live in a pastoral and agricultural society where time honoured crafts and homely pastimes are pursued and enjoyed, affected only by the changing seasons and immemorial tradition. We live in a world dominated by scientific and technological change and invention, and we live dangerously. We cannot even feed and clothe ourselves or fuel our homes and machines from our own native resources. Our primary products are few and we survive by our skills in commerce, industry and technology. Industrialization has brought us benefits. Wealth has been redistributed so that the majority are more affluent and our growing technology has contributed to immense increases in leisure and the means and opportunities to enjoy it. In so complex a society the need for more men to read and to read better than men have read before increases as knowledge grows apace. Previously useful knowledge is discarded and new learning is required to replace the old. It is not just that new knowledge replaces old on a straight one to one basis. New learning and new skills tend to be much more complex than the simpler ones that are replaced, and knowledge of the innovations grows at a frightening pace, necessitating constant relearning and retraining and infinite flexibility and powers of adaptation. Even increased leisure has brought a demand for increased reading. People with newly acquired interests and the capital invested in them represented by cars, yachts, fishing gear, golf clubs and the like want to learn how to improve their performance and enjoyment of their hobbies and possessions. Increased leisure has also made possible the 'do it yourself' phenomenon which shows no sign of abating, nor does the vast quantity of 'do it yourself' literature which has grown (and continues to grow rapidly) to accommodate such a multitude of enthusiasts. Television, frequently maligned by the bibliophile as the cause of some decline in literacy, has in fact led to a massive growth in reading as the compelling communications industry introduces a vast public to new interests. Reading is far from in decline as each year sees more books printed and sold than any year before. Society wants more books to make the culture more satisfying. The demand comes from the people – the publishers merely supply it.

It may be that television and other devices such as the family car have led to less reading of fiction than was formerly the case. These days reading for pleasure has to compete with a number of other pleasures which greater affluence and leisure have made possible. This does not necessarily mean that less reading is being done. Without doubt, very much more is being done and has proved to be very necessary, but it is being done in different ways and for different purposes. However, it would be a poor teacher of reading who would not consider the enjoyment of a good book as at least the equal of the more synthetic products of the entertainment industry. It would appear to me to be a retrograde step to concede to television the custody and transmission of worthwhile tastes and the whole cultural heritage which literature enshrines. Fortunately there appears to be little likelihood of this happening. The reader is in much more active control of his book than the television watcher is of his programme. He has a power of almost universal selection of material, can use his material for numerous purposes in a variety of ways, can read at times and in places of his own choosing, and can vary the pace of intensity of his activity at will. The viewer, apart from having the power of switching on or off, can do little to accommodate to the material provided from a limited number of channels but control its volume and clarity of definition. There is no substitute for reading. It remains second only to speech as the major means of communication. Unfortunately it is not acquired naturally as speech is for the majority. It is a learned skill and therefore it has to be taught. The earlier it is learned and the better it is taught the more our children will have opportunities to live fuller and richer lives in what has come to be a reading world.

References

START, K. B. and WELLS, B. K. (1972) *The Trend of Reading Standards* Slough: NFER

Chapter 2

The bases of early reading

How do small children learn to read? The question is unanswerable because two questions fundamental to it remain unanswered: what is involved in the actual process of beginning reading? what factors within children cause them to learn to read most effectively? These questions remain unanswered despite the fact that of all aspects of the curriculum reading has been and continues to be the object of the widest and most thorough-going research. There remain methods and materials. The innovations have not given, and cannot give, any guarantee of success because their inventors have had no firm base of a general theory of reading on which to establish practice. In the absence of a suitable theoretical framework, innovations arise from intuition only. Despite lack of knowledge on the part of educators, the apparently miraculous feat of learning to read is constantly achieved by millions of small children. The teacher's difficulties are compounded by the fact that many children learn to read in conditions which the majority of educators regard as impossible, while on the other hand ideal conditions produce a disturbingly large number of reading failures. What is emerging from observation and research, drawing upon a number of disciplines which include sociology, psychology, linguistics and psycholinguistics, is a view of reading which holds it to be far less of the simple perceptual skill it has been thought to be and much more a complex blend of the most intricate workings of the mind which identify it more closely with thinking than with any other human ability. But this is merely to consider reading as a process – the 'how' of reading. The 'what' of reading is a system of communication, analogous to speaking, dependent on it, and yet certainly different from it. The act of early reading involves the marrying of both process and system to the child, and although all three constantly interact and interrelate, it might be fruitful to consider each element separately and in some detail.

The process of reading
Firstly, I would like to make it clear that I regard as fruitless discussion as to whether reading is merely simple decoding or a much more complex

set of operations which may involve evaluation, interpretation, and many other so-called higher order skills. I regard as reading both decoding and the kind of reading that may be described as critical or as reflective. I do not consider decoding as reading when understanding or meaning do not result. This is merely to translate from one set of symbols or code to another, both codes being equally incomprehensible to the learner. Decoding may be at a lowly, purely literal level of comprehension, but it will be reading if the decoder acquires from his code-breaking the meaning the author intended him to receive. Therefore reading is decoding for meaning and can occur on a continuum anywhere between very simple and very complex.

Reading begins with the perception of printed symbols. For most people the perception is associated with seeing, but the blind perceive the symbols by touch. The perceptions transmitted to the brain by the nervous system cause a series of mental reactions to occur. If recognition of the words represented by the perceived symbols occurs, reading can be said to have begun. Recognition will not be possible unless the word represented by the symbol is familiar. At the first introduction to print, when the attack skills of the beginner are minimal and the operation of the few strategies available to him fail to make the word meaningful because of its unfamiliarity, reading cannot be said to occur. At the very beginning of reading it is essential that all the words to be read are within the spoken vocabulary of the reader so that recognition may lead to comprehension. A number of other mental processes will almost certainly need to be brought into operation in order to comprehend even the simplest sentence. Where one or more of the words has more than one meaning, some process of selection has to operate to assign the correct meaning. Selection depends upon the efficiency of the long-term memory in storing up words acquired from previous experiences or associations, and also upon the efficiency of the retrieval system involved in digging words out and applying them correctly. Correct application depends upon the operation of an evaluation mechanism which monitors the selections in order to assign meaning most appropriately i.e. in context. As each new perception sets in train the mental processes described, it is necessary simultaneously to retain within the short-term memory abstracts of the meaning of the previous percepts in order to make sense of even the simplest sentence. As sentence follows sentence, the essence of previous sentences has to be distilled by a process of ever increasing abstraction and retained sequentially until the current paragraph is completed, all this simultaneously with the processing of new perceptions. Finally, in order to understand even the most simply constructed story, the details must be processed by organizational mechanisms into a coherent whole. In attempting to thus model the reading process I have had in mind the minimum of mental organization required to read a story of the level of, say, *The Gingerbread Boy* or *The Three Bears*. No attempt has been made to categorize or indicate the many more numerous and complex mental abilities required for critical, interpretative or study reading. Even so, reading at the simplest level can be seen to be a complex interaction of coordinated mental processes, executed with great rapidity, and usually quite unconsciously. The ingredients of the model are three-fold:

1 Perceptual skill.
2 Thinking ability.
3 A pool of words, concepts and experience (total oral language background) on which the beginner can draw. Without this the processing of printed symbols would stop at perception. Recognition could not even begin.

Reading as a communication system
Reading differs from the other language skills of speaking and writing because of its decoding component, that is, the necessity to translate written symbols into sound. The translation process is made difficult for small children by the very nature of the graphic symbols employed. Letters may be of different sizes and forms according to whether they are printed or written, capital or lower case. A variety of type faces are in common use. A change in orientation can transform 6 into 9, n into u, and b into d, p or q.

Some of the difficulties small children face when first confronted with the conventions involved in cracking the reading code may be brought home by the following simulation. Let us suppose that I tell you that I have invented a new language and that I challenge you to read the following word: X 1 X = + X : − / i V. You confess to having difficulty so I try to give you confidence by pointing out that at least the symbols are familiar to you and that the signs represent some of the letters in your own language, and that the characters are even simpler than those to which you are accustomed as they are made up of straight lines and dots and have no curves. I might add that you have advantages in this situation which the small child learning to read has not. You are familiar with the terms symbol, sign, language, letters and characters. The beginner starting school may be familiar with the terms line, dot, straight and curved, but probably not in the context of description of printed characters. You are also familiar with all the symbols used – many a child starting school will not be familiar with any of the printed symbols in which his language is written. However, none of my remarks seems to be helping you, so to make it easier I translate my symbols into their equivalent letter forms in your own language. Thus you have:

SISATSQEMOH.

Your knowledge of grapheme/phoneme correspondence and the rules of syllabification (knowledge not available to the neophyte in reading) enables you to put together a series of sounds which result in a 'word' unrecognizable to you. I then apologize for having forgotten to tell you in the first place that my new language was originally devised for left-handed children who, in my experience, have difficulty in writing curves (hence the dots and straight lines) and who appear to find it easier to read from right to left. Apologizing once again, I then rearrange the symbols in what are to you the conventional left to right sequence. Thus you have the word

HOMEOSTASIS.

You make a creditable attempt at sounding it but confess that although it sounds like a proper word, it is one of which you have had no previous experience or for which you cannot find any known associations. You have made the right noises, you have 'barked at the print' but have not even begun to read it because you have not achieved the first requisite of reading, namely recognition. You have not decoded it. You have recoded it from one set of symbols to another, equally incomprehensible from the point of view of meaning.

I now try to help you in a big way and drop you a broad hint about the way in which many of the words of English have their roots in one or other of the so-called classical languages. You remark that this is no help to you as in your first year at grammar school the classics mistress eloped with the caretaker and was never replaced. I decide to give you an enormous clue and ask if you have had any training in medicine or psychology. No, you say, you are training to be a teacher. I resist the temptation to tut tut and to advise you to take your psychology more seriously. Instead I now fall over backwards to help you, short of actually telling you what the word means. I produce an article in which the word appears in context. Unfortunately it is written by a psychiatrist for other psychiatrists, who are of course both doctors and psychologists, and the writer assumes that his readers have a background of concepts on which understanding of the article can be based. It is too specialized for you to make anything of the context. But you are determined not to be beaten. You dash out of the room and return with a dictionary, which not only tells you what homeostasis means but how to pronounce it. You finally won but had to admit that, despite your long experience of language as speaker, listener, reader and writer and the application of sophisticated skills far beyond those available to the tiny beginner, you were unable to read the word from your own unaided linguistic resources. You had to use a very advanced ability (dictionary skills) which five or six year olds rarely possess.

This attempt to put the teacher on level terms with children first confronted with the problems associated with beginning reading serves to remind us that reading has unique difficulties which do not arise in that more natural and more easily acquired form of communication – speech. It is possible for someone to know the letters and still be unable to synthesize them into words and, as the simulation has attempted to show, it is possible to make up words and still be unable to assign meaning to them. In the case of direct communication by speech the listener does not have to translate writing into sound but frequently has additional positive assistance from the speaker by means of gesture, facial expression, intonation and stress. It is possible for two speakers of different nationalities, neither of whom knows the other's language, to communicate to each other feelings of joy, hate, fear, disdain and the like and even to negotiate quite complicated financial transactions, and to give and receive directions entirely by signs. Print offers to the beginner no such props to meaning.

The dilemma for the teacher of beginning reading is to decide to what extent reading is to be considered a set of skills which can be taught and tested. The simulation showed that there was no lack of skills on the part of the would-be reader. His failure was due to an inadequate background of appropriate language concepts. This, as was indicated when considering reading as a process, seems to be a fundamental requirement before reading can begin. Skills can profitably be taught, but only on a basis of adequately developed oral language and experience.

The child as potential reader

In order to overcome the unique difficulties inherent in beginning reading it is necessary for the child to have first developed a minimum set of skills and capacities. The paramount importance of a basis of concepts acquired through experience and supported by oral language facility has been repeatedly stressed. As the level of language development acquired by children starting school will be almost entirely dependent on the child-rearing practices adopted by parents, it is important for teachers of beginning reading to study the determinants of early language growth. Many of the factors affecting preschool language are beyond the powers of teachers to influence or control. Nevertheless, teachers need to be aware of preschool language determinants in order to make appropriate compensation for linguistic deficiency. The growth of nursery provision also points to the possibility of greater opportunities for teachers to influence parental child-rearing practice by encouraging parent participation in school activities and by direct education, both explicit and implicit, of parents who are brought within the influence of school much earlier than was formerly possible. In other words, we can catch the children younger and more positively influence parents sooner than we have ever been able to do before.

The earliest language babies hear is uttered by their mothers. It is almost always accompanied by love and comfort. The newborn baby's wants are few. He sleeps most of the time. He wakes when he is hungry, wet, has soiled his nappy, or has wind. On each of these occasions his mother relieves his distress and provides a bonus of warm physical contact by suckling, fondling, nursing, dandling and kissing accompanied by soothing words. Thus early language is associated with warmth, love and affection. To most mothers the giving of affection comes naturally, but in certain cases love and the time and opportunity to demonstrate it are lacking. When this happens the baby's physical wants may be satisfied but inadequately accompanied by affective language. Thus when the child's first experimental babblings and gurglings meet no affective response, when he has no responsive models for imitation and practice, and no encouragement in his first strivings to communicate, the urge to communicate is stifled in the first few months of life. Such early stifling of the communication drive results in rapid withdrawal from social contact and stimulation, and later attempts to revive it almost invariably fail. Bowlby, who should be required reading for all students of child development, has most thoroughly documented the effects of maternal deprivation and neglect in the first few months of life (Bowlby 1964). The commonest causes of linguistic failure in early infancy are the death, serious illness or hospitalization of the mother or the hospitalization of the baby himself. Others, which if cumulative can be no less serious in their effects on the child, are the frustrations influencing the mother due to poverty, poor living conditions and overcrowding, which affect both the quality and provision (especially time available) of affective situations between mother and child, and emotional and personality disturbances which prevent the mother from giving her baby the love and affection which he needs. Physical factors such as blindness, deafness, spasticity or brain damage resulting from childbirth or accident also affect the baby's ability to respond to the language stimulation provided by the mother.

Social class and economic factors undoubtedly influence the quality of early mother–child relationships. The mother who is financially well endowed, has her quota of labour-saving devices, can afford some domestic help and whose husband takes his share of family chores and participates in child rearing, can devote more time and attention to her baby than the hard-pressed mother whose every act is at sheer survival level.

As the baby grows in his ability to reproduce the language he hears around him, the range and power of his repertoire is influenced by the quality of the oral language background which pervades the home. Other adults – father and relations – and siblings provide models for imitation and emulation, and give support, encouragement, praise and stimulation. Social and economic factors continue to affect the power of the family to provide the necessary conditions for development. Basic requirements such as food, clothing, warmth, fresh air, sleep and dental and medical care need to be supplemented by suitable provision of toys, play facilities and challenging stimuli and experiences which promote emotional development affecting interest, effort and confidence. The child's power to respond to challenge starts from feelings of stability, security and dependence. He grows towards independence by careful parental monitoring and variation of challenging situations which are within his power to accomplish. Support, praise and encouragement should attend each new achievement or recklessness or excessive timidity rather than confidence may result.

As children reach the questioning stage the amount of time and interest which parents devote to their children most profoundly affects the growth of language. How many mothers sit with their small children and religiously watch children's television programmes and then follow up their viewing with discussion and exploitation of ideas and activities arising from the programme? How many parents faithfully read the bedtime story each evening at the appointed time, explain the pictures in the book and encourage the child to comment and ask questions? How many parents patiently answer all their children's questions and go out of their way to discuss their interests, to play and to talk? How many fathers resist the temptation to miss the match on a Saturday but instead take the children to the zoo, to a castle, for walks in the country or by the sea, and share their pleasure in the discovery of new words, concepts, ideas and interests? The more selfless parents are in doing these and similar things, the more they will be rewarded by the growing liveliness of their children. And when their children start school early reading will soon be within their grasp.

Social class to a great extent influences the capacity to illuminate experience by the use of language. Bernstein (1971) sees language as the reflection of social class conditioning. The middle classes and those with middle class aspirations and attitudes find many and varied uses for language – exploration of ideas and problems, description, social and business intercourse. Their children, growing up in a rich language background, unconsciously absorb the varied language patterns they constantly hear. The lower working classes tend to concentrate on objects rather than ideas. They find abstractions harder to cope with. Their language patterns and the uses to which they put them are more limited. They keep their language to a minimum, assume that their hearers know what they are talking about and fall back on nods, winks and facial expressions when words can be avoided. Bernstein describes the language of the lower working class as a restricted code, that of the middle classes as elaborated.

A number of observers have followed up Bernstein's work. In one experiment I gave a group of children the following task: 'You are playing rounders. The ball goes through a window. Tell about this.'

A typical lower working class response was as follows: 'We was playing. Billy hit it. It went through a window. This feller comes out. So we run off.' The author kept strictly to the bare bones of the story without elaboration. There are no adjectives or adverbs. Tenses are confused. The author assumed that his reader knew the game that 'we was playing' and that I knew what the 'it' was that Billy hit. He omitted to mention whether the window was open or closed and assumed again that I jolly well knew that the window was broken. The possibility that the window may not actually have been broken did not occur to him and therefore the possibility of certain other consequences did not arise. There was no attempt to set the scene, time or other circumstances and no description of people, incidents or feelings.

A response typical of the middle class children in the group went thus: 'It was too late when I had finished my homework to go to the park. So my younger sister Elizabeth, who is eight, and I called for Stephanie and Mark, the twins who live next door. They are both ten, a year younger than I. We decided to play rounders in our garden. Unfortunately the game did not last long because Mark gave the ball an enormous hit and broke an upstairs window in Mr Taylor's house. We were very surprised because the ball was very soft and light. Mr Taylor did not come out but we decided we had better knock and apologize. Mr Taylor did not know we had broken the window. He is a bit deaf and had been watching television and had not heard anything. He went upstairs to look at the damage and when he came down he gave us back our ball. He told us not to worry about the window. It was already cracked and he had been meaning to have a new one put in for a long time.'

This account indicates that the young author had a good idea of what she thought I would want when I set the task. She gives a complete account, filling in all the details, and connects them into a coherent, syntactical whole. She is obviously at ease with words and sensitive to the uses to which language can be put.

I have also observed mothers of different social classes with their children in the local supermarket. It is fascinating to see how a typical middle class mother reacts to her children's comments and questions. The views of the children, however small, are treated like those of other intelligent adults. There is no attempt to condescend, to talk down, or to shut the child up. The mother is unconsciously teaching the child the whole time, especially by the detailed explanations she gives whenever there seems to her to be need. The conversation between mothers and children of the lower working class consists largely of questions and requests from the children which are met in the main by negations, prohibitions, and commands, devoid of explanation, from the mother, for example:

'No, you can't have Sugar Puffs.'
'Why, mum?'
'Now, didn't I just say no?'
'Yes, but –'
'Well I mean it. And put that down!'
'Why mum?'
' 'Cos I said so. Put it down and come on!'

It is not that the mother is necessarily brusque or short tempered or lacking in patience; rather is it that her own uses for language are limited to what is strictly practical or useful.

Other factors, not necessarily related to social class, affect the development of preschool language. Bilingualism in families, especially when the mother is non-English speaking, may limit the growth of vocabulary, ideas and concepts, particularly when opportunities for play and social contact with English speaking children are slight. Immigration, frequently accompanied by social segregation, poses similar but even more serious problems, especially for newly arrived families from underdeveloped countries whose cultures are markedly different from ours. Size of family also affects early language growth. When children are numerous it becomes difficult for mothers to devote adequate time and attention to children at critical stages in the language growth process. Younger children are particularly disadvantaged here. Successful language development depends on close and frequent linguistic contact with adults. When there is a large number of children the youngest is most frequently in contact with the next child up and it is the responsibility of older sisters to feed, dress, take him to school and the like. Consequently, not only do younger children have insufficient linguistic intercourse with adults, they also tend to be more dependent on siblings than do first-born children in smaller

families. Size of family and parental attitude also help to determi
social climate which results from family organization. In a well-org
household, breakfast and other mealtimes provide daily opportuni
contact with adult language. One can contrast the breakfast time when
both parents sit down to table with their children and discuss the weather,
the news and forthcoming school events with that in the home where the
father rarely sees his children at mealtimes and where the working mother
often delegates the organization of meals to older children. Parental
temperament also influences the use to which children put language. The
children of overdemanding parents are often shy and hesitant and with-
draw from challenges such as learning to read. Children may be overindulged and lack the determination required to begin reading. Children
vary in their developmental pattern. The child who is slow in learning to
talk is usually slow in learning to read. Very low intelligence also deters
the growth of language, although children of low intelligence often have
little or no difficulty in learning to read when they are emotionally stable
and keen to learn. Motivation to read is obviously low in homes that have
few books and where the parents are seen to have little use for, and derive
little pleasure from books. Often in cases where children are linguistically,
physically, socially and emotionally mature a last minute setback can put
them off reading at crucial times in the important early stages. In my
experience the commonest cause of this is the arrival of a new baby
coinciding with a sibling starting school. The child, who for five years has
been the centre of the domestic universe, unconsciously suffers extreme
emotional deflation when his mother's love is apparently suddenly
transferred to a newcomer. His sense of loss is made even more acute by
starting school which seems to him an additional deliberate act of rejection
on the part of his mother.

The very numerous possibilities of early linguistic deprivation make it
necessary for nursery/infant teachers to be adept at recording the all-round
growth of children in the fullest possible way, both by acquiring from
parents and others relevant information and by their own sensitive
observation of indicators which children themselves exhibit. The major
problem which the nursery/infant teacher faces is how to reproduce for
all children in school conditions, the rich language background in which
the more fortunate children naturally grow.

References
BERNSTEIN, B. (1971) *Class Codes and Control* London: Routledge and
    Kegan Paul
BOWLBY, J. (1964) *Child Care and the Growth of Love* Harmondsworth:
    Penguin

Chapter 3

Training in visual skills

For the majority of people, reading starts with seeing. The brain receives the perceptions and if what is perceived is what the author intended to be perceived, i.e. if accurate recognition occurs, reading can be said to have begun. How children are trained at the earliest stages to register print depends on the philosophy of the teacher and the working model of beginning reading on which she depends. Teachers concerned with the formal beginning of reading can be classified into two groups: those who depend on whole word (look and say) methods and those who start by teaching the children the letters in order that they may synthesize them into words (phonic methods). In the latter case what actually happens is that the word to be read is broken down into its constituent letters, i.e. is analysed, before the synthesis can occur. In practice, the vast majority of teachers in England and Wales introduce recognition by whole word methods. When a substantial sight vocabulary has been established, some phonic work is begun, and hence such an approach can be called an eclectic one. In Scotland teachers are much more likely to adopt phonic methods from the outset and only use look and say methods for words where phonic conventions do not apply. The preliminaries to recognition will differ therefore according to whether one favours phonic or whole word methods. Where phonic methods predominate, prereading visual work will aim at discrimination of separate letter shapes. Exponents of whole word methods will put the emphasis on discriminating between word patterns. In either case the majority of children starting school will require some training in visual discrimination.

The vision of most children nearly old enough to start school is adequate for their everyday purposes. They can see (and also, if necessary, handle, taste, smell and hear) the concrete objects which make up their environment. They do not have to rely only on vision in order to interpret the world around them. On their introduction to reading they are confronted (for many children for the very first time) by abstract symbols which have no a parent relationship with objects in the real world, and which are quite unrelated to anything within their previous experience.

To interpret them they have to rely almost entirely on vision. The printed symbols, whether separate letters or words, are extremely minute compared with almost all other objects of which they have experience. Consequently, the task of reading calls for the ability to make very fine discriminations of a kind which the majority of five year olds are quite unaccustomed to making. Hence some attention to visual discrimination will need to be given to almost all children as part of prereading activity. The amount of such training required will vary according to the different aptitudes of the children being taught, but as aptitude stems from both genetic endowment and the interaction of the environmental influences to which individuals are exposed, one can only conclude that the needs of any one child will never be precisely the same as those of another. This does not necessarily mean that the teaching of visual discrimination skills needs to be entirely individualized. We must assume in a normal distribution a considerable cluster about the mean. What we must also assume, however, is that towards the lower extreme of the distribution there will be children of such low aptitude that the widest possible progression of carefully graded exercises in visual discrimination will need to be experienced.

The basis of look and say methods is that the child learns, by frequent repetition, to recognize the visual patterns of which words are formed. Most look and say primers try to avoid confusion by presenting words of dissimilar shape in close proximity. The theory behind this is that to present a sentence such as 'Pat had a fat cat' is to force on the child the need to make unnecessarily difficult discriminations by including three words – Pat, had and fat – of quite similar shape so close together. The assumption is that the child does not see the separate letters but receives a global impression of a word, say 'Pat', which, because it consists of two ascenders separated by a small vowel, would be registered mentally as

If this is so then Pat, had and fat all have the same shape. To the look and say theorist the sentence quoted would be one of great complexity because of the confusingly similar shapes of the component words which might be perceived thus:

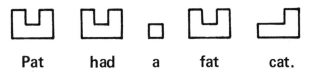

Pat   had   a   fat   cat.

The look and say exponent would regard a sentence such as 'The monkey runs up the tree' as simple because of the varied patterns made by the word shapes in the group. These would be registered thus:

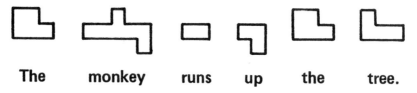

The   monkey   runs   up   the   tree.

Those who favour look and say approaches would probably point out that not only is 'The monkey runs up the tree' a much simpler visual exercise than 'Pat had a fat cat', but also that it is psychologically simpler because of its greater interest value. Personally I can see no justification for either assumption. To the child trained in phonics 'Pat had a fat cat' is a simple business involving the blending of only six consonants with the open vowel 'a', whereas the same sentence might well be the simple prelude to a very exciting story indeed. One cannot judge the interest value of a story by only one of the sentences in it. Exponents of look and say methods lay great stress on the interest value of words chosen in early reading matter. Unfortunately the heavy reliance placed on the need for repetition drastically reduces the interest level of the material. One can imagine the typical look and say primer page which might read thus:

The monkey runs up the tree.
See the monkey run up the tree.
Up the tree the monkey runs.
Up. Up. Up.

We do not know how children actually see the words presented to them and there seems little doubt that different children see words in different ways, but it does seem unfortunate that many teachers have accepted so uncritically the word shape theory postulated by Schonell in 1942. If children do indeed see the word 'Pat' as

then it would be quite impossible for them to make sense of any reading matter involving words of similar shape at all. Schonell did, of course, qualify his theory of total word pattern by pointing out that the total pattern is influenced by word length, distinctive projections formed by ascenders and descenders, and groupings such as familiar letter strings. However, even this does not justify the assumption that the final impression is a geometric shape only. My own experience is that the most important clue on which beginners seize is the first letter of a word and as my experience is supported by that of a great number of teachers with whom I have discussed the problem, I am continually surprised at the reluctance of look and say enthusiasts to ascribe any importance to the learning of letter shapes (and sounds) as an aid to recognition at the very beginnings of reading.

If children are not taught their letters they are naturally going to have difficulty with short words which are to them of apparently similar shape. It is my experience (and one which has been borne out in discussions with over a hundred reception class teachers) that beginning readers most easily and accurately recognize short words, despite similarity of length and overall shape, *provided they have been taught their letters.* Obviously they will have difficulty with longer words because of their limited focussing and fixatory powers. The trained or experienced adult reader has learned to make swift and economical eye movements in order to process the printed word. His eyes move in a left to right direction along a line of print and at the end of each line make a swift backward and downward sweep to the beginning of the next line. The eyes cannot see while they are moving and so their left to right progress along each line of print is not a continuous movement but one of fits and starts, that is of short movements and pauses. The pauses are known as fixations and it is only during the fixations that reading occurs. At the start of each fixation the eyes see by first focussing on one small area and then fanning out rapidly in all directions. At first all that is seen clearly is the centre of the initial focus but this soon widens out to include the print on either side. At the extremes of the focus there is a blur. The length of print that can be seen clearly during each fixation is known as the visual span and this can be increased by practice and experience. The eyes pause on average between four and ten times, depending on visual span, along a line of ordinary length. People differ in the number of pauses they need to make and, therefore, in their speed of reading. Individuals vary not only in the number of fixations they make per line, but also in the time spent on each fixation. The duration of the pauses will depend on the difficulty level of different types of material. Very interesting or familiar material is usually processed in very short fixations. As reading matter increases in difficulty the pauses tend to be longer as well as more numerous. Therefore, the beginning reader, whose visual span is limited, is more likely to take in a short word in one fixation than he is a long word. When confronted with a long word the beginner may have to make several fixations and in so moving he may easily 'lose his place'. If this happens because long words are introduced too early and too frequently, eye movements may become regressive right at the very beginning of reading and the development of smooth left to right eye movements may be impeded. Hence from the visual point of view alone, early reading matter should consist of short words which are within the child's spoken vocabulary. The misconception that beginning readers do not have difficulty with big words arises from the fact that, in some well known primers, words such as 'elephant' and 'aeroplane' happen to be the only long words in an entire book. When these same words are placed in groups of words of similar length and configuration they are rarely recognized.

I believe that to give children training in whole-word pattern discrimination has little value. How could one train a child to read 'Pat' for

when the same shape applies to 'fat', 'had' and quite a number of other words? The permutations are numerous indeed when any combination of ascenders other than P and t is substituted. It is the patterns within words on which we could more usefully concentrate. For example, in the sentence 'Pat had a fat cat' the most consistent pattern is the 'at' in Pat, fat and cat. Training the children to look for such consistent relationships (patterns) plus initial letter shapes and sounds is much more economical than having the children learn every single word in isolation. Unless the children are used to detecting similarities and differences in language patterns they will never become fluent readers, but will read word by word because they have been taught no attack skills which enable them to see relationships. Ability to detect similarities enables them to note that Pat, fat and cat all end with symbols 'at' which correspond to a certain sound. To differentiate between the words all that is needed is the ability to recognize that the initial letters are different and that each is allied to a particular sound. Ability to detect differences also prevents children from confusing words of similar shape. For example, the child who knows 'at' in Pat, fat and cat is unlikely to confuse Pat with Pot.

Some difficulties in visual perception

A great deal of traditional prereading activity centres on sorting (detection of differences) and matching (detecting similarities). What we must be certain of is the purpose behind such activity. It has been suggested that in the first place activity should be directed towards training the children in nitial letter shapes (and sounds) and in the detection of consistent shape (and sound) patterns within words. There are a number of difficulties inherent in these processes. Orientation is a major one. A normal four year old will readily recognize a dog as a dog whether it is sitting, lying down or standing. Letters in print are composed of straight lines or curves or combinations of both. A change in orientation can transform b into d, p or q. Considerable powers of discrimination are therefore required to master the orientations involved in reading accurately the words bad, dad, pad. Minute differences separate n from h and n from r; 6 and 9 and u and n are straight reversals. Differences in type forms add to confusion. The children may be used to seeing a and g as the accepted forms on the blackboard and in their own early writing but may see those same characters represented as a and g in printed books. Sixteen of the capital letters have different shapes from their lower case counterparts, and at least one capital letter will be encountered in every sentence to be read.

From concrete to abstract
To lead the children from experience of concrete objects only to the ability to interpret abstract symbols is a complex task. Graded exercises in sorting and matching have been the traditional intuitive response of teachers to the problem. I know of no certain evidence of transfer of skill in sorting and matching to success in discriminating between letter shapes and word patterns. However, the general theory of concept development indicates that categorization is the first stage in the process of abstraction. For example, if the first large animal in a child's experience is a horse, all big quadrupeds are likely to be similarly named until the child gradually comes to recognize the distinguishing characteristics by which quadrupeds are categorized. The attributes which most commonly aid categorization are those of shape, size, colour, texture and function. The child, if helped, soon learns to distinguish, by the presence or absence of certain characteristics, between horse, cow, cat and dog. By a process of increasing powers of differentiation he can come to categorize within the genus 'horse' such subcategories as stallion, mare, colt, filly, race-horse and pony, while the idea of horse, the generic term, applies to all members of the species. In order to hold this concept the child has to discern the differences by which the subcategories are identified as well as the common factors by which they are related. The child can now be said to have acquired the abstract concept of 'horse', whereas to begin with the horse was one particular horse, say the horse in the field next door and no other. The idea 'horse' is an abstraction derived by a long process of differentiation and the establishment of ideas of relationship starting from the one real, concrete,

horse within his experience. Children learn to establish number concepts and relationships by a similar process of abstraction from concrete starting points. If children cannot distinguish between concrete three-dimensional objects in the real world they will certainly have difficulty with the intangible shapes of print.

Practical work in visual discrimination

The most commonly used concrete sorting and matching materials are beads. These can be bought, usually in boxes of 100, from most educational suppliers. The commonest shapes are 'round' beads (spheres) and cubes. Both can be ordered in cross-sections of $1''$, $\frac{1}{2}''$ and $\frac{1}{4}''$ in each of four colours – red, blue, yellow and green. Given a few sorting boxes (egg boxes are useful here) and an assortment of beads, the children can order these by size, shape or colour, or in any combination of these. The beads can also be arranged in numerical groupings. Thus can be learned the names of the colours (a feat of which many children are incapable when they start school). The children can also acquire, by handling as well as by seeing, an understanding of important basic words such as round, square, cube, small, big, bigger, biggest, more, less, same and different. Similar practice can be acquired by threading the beads in simply graded pattern arrangements. This activity is particularly valuable in the development of number concepts and relationships. When the children can thread bead strings in patterns of some complexity it is useful for the teacher to have a number of bead string patterns of her own permanently available. These should be graded from very simple to very complex and each should contain a deliberate error, an odd one which breaks the sequence or arrangement and which the children should be encouraged, by observation and discussion, to identify. Collections of buttons are also useful for sorting and matching activity.

Similar work can be done with ribbons and assorted strips of coloured card. If card is used it should be given a transparent protective covering. Ribbons are particularly useful for teaching the idea of tints. A good set of ribbons would include the colours white, black, grey, brown, red, yellow and green. They should be graded by size, say $10''$, $8''$, $6''$ and $4''$ in order to familiarize the children with basic terms such as little, short, shorter, shortest, long, longer, longest, same and different. The children can acquire some familiarity with tints if each length category of ribbon is presented in three shades – dark, mid and pale – of the major colours. Thus the child can learn new dimensions of colour by acquiring understanding of words such as dark, medium, light and pale, and can thus increase his powers of classification.

Work with beads, buttons, ribbons and the like, which is important in developing awareness of the importance of shape, size, colour, texture and number as distinguishing characteristics, is often supplemented by materials which can add a functional attribute to those already listed. Many teachers find that collections of *Matchbox* and *Dinky* model vehicles which can be categorized into saloons, vans, sports cars, and farm vehicles, each of which can be ordered into subcategories by size and colour, are particularly interesting to children. One reception class teacher has a collection of model creatures which the children sort into categories such as domestic birds and animals, and wild or zoo creatures. One particularly inventive friend of mine prepares a different tray each day and presents a number of apparently discrete objects which the children are invited to order into groups by observation and discussion. One of the children's favourite trays is that on which the objects can be classified as 'things we eat', 'things we eat with' and 'things we drink'. Another of my acquaintances takes the children on leaf-gathering walks. On their return the children classify the finds into leaf families.

Practical work at more abstract levels

When the children have had ample practice in sorting and matching at a concrete level by handling, observing and discussing, using real objects usually of a three-dimensional kind, they are then introduced to material which, though still easily handled, is flat (i.e. two-dimensional) and more abstract (less representational) than the objects used in previous work. Philip and Tacey Limited produce some useful material of this type. Their profile counters, which represent profiles of common objects like butterflies, cars and trains, are very attractive. A feature of this material is the number of different shape–colour combinations that can be made. The profile counters can be usefully followed up by the easily handled but more abstract pattern making materials, *Tri-Pat* and *Multi-Pat*, also produced by Philip and Tacey. As well as being attractive this material is durable and is supplied in strong, compact boxes. I find this material much more easy to organize than Fuzzy-felt, which lends itself to similar activities, but which is somewhat messy to distribute, control and collect.

There is a long tradition in prereading activity of giving the children practice in pattern making and recognition. The theory which underlies such activity is that letter shapes and word patterns have constancy as well as similarity in form. Thus b, d, p and q, which are all combinations of l and o (a stick and a ring) are differentiated by the distinctive patterns in which the component sticks and rings are organized. Not only must the child learn the distinctive patterns of the straight lines and curves and combinations of these by which each letter is recognized, he must also acquire the concept of the constancy of the letter forms. Thus he must learn that the d in dog is the same letter (i.e. has the same shape and sound) as the d in dig. Without such awareness the child would not be able to apply his knowledge of letter shapes and sounds to the various word patterns which he meets and would not gain independence in blending or in word analysis when confronted with new vocabulary. In the same way the idea of constancy of word patterns must also be conceptualized. In order to achieve minimal fluency the reader must recognize that the meaning associated with the pattern of symbols 'dog' will be the same regardless of the line or page in which the word recurs. It is here that the variety of letter forms in common use can cause problems. For example, the word 'dog' can be rendered dog, **dog**, DOG, **Dog** or Dog. My own solution to part of this problem is to protect the children from all forms of print in which **g** is represented as g until they have sufficient reading experience to conceptualize the less familiar shape. Capital letters need not cause difficulty if the children are taught from the very beginning that every letter has two shapes: the big letter (capital) and the little letter (lower case). For a time some odd varieties of word forms will characterize the children's early attempts at writing. 'Cat', for example, may appear variously as CAT, CAt, Cat, cAt, cAT or caT, but these are all linguistically correct and ensure that writing reinforces reading performance from the outset. As the children acquire both implicitly and explicitly a growing understanding of the rules of capitalization, a more orthodox version of written forms will ensue. However, it is generally acknowledged that if children lack experience in detecting the similarities and differences by which patterns of a concrete nature are made and recognized, they will certainly have difficulty in the recognition (reading) and the construction (writing) of the more abstract patterns made by letters, syllables and words in print.

Teachers have traditionally placed great faith in jigsaw puzzles, constructional toys and the like as aids to the recognition and construction of patterns within words, e.g. the 'at' common to Pat, fat and cat. The underlying theory, if such intuitive judgments can indeed merit the term theory, is that before the child can acquire expertise in recognizing and forming relationships between parts and wholes in words which are themselves abstractions, he must have prior experience of the seeing of relationships in more concrete and representational situations. Though I know of no research which points to a positive correlation between ability with jigsaw puzzles and early reading success, my personal experience is that I have never known a child who has great ability with jigsaws to have difficulty with reading. Nor have I ever known a child who has difficulty with jigsaw puzzles tackle reading with any facility. The reasons for this may go quite beyond the obvious perceptual skill of matching a shape to a hole and may depend for its transfer value, as does so much of the visual training in prereading, more on the accompanying oral activity than on the purely visual. However, the traditional approach, which I would personally support, is that graded practice with jigsaw puzzles provides important experience, which the home background of many children does not supply or reinforce, in judging, evaluating and seeing relationships between parts and wholes. The experience is all the more valuable if the first jigsaws are large and simple, maximum twelve pieces, and childproof. It helps, especially from the point of view of distribution and collection, if the back of each puzzle is separately colour-coded or otherwise rendered easily identifiable, and if children handling them are working in one small group at a time. I have known student teachers who are overenthusiastic about having large numbers of children occupied with a great variety of jigsaws, to be faced with a frightening chaos of jumbled pieces at clearing-up time, in comparison with which Hercules's task of clearing up the Augean stables was a relatively simple matter. In the same category as jigsaw puzzles, especially for the establishment of relationships between means and ends and between parts and wholes, come the constructional toys of which Lego is the least messy and most popular with small children. Again, whether the transfer, and my own experience is that there is positive transfer between constructional and reading ability, is due to the visual experience acquired or to the functional application of oral language with which the activity is usually accompanied, or to the combination of both, is a matter which researchers have yet to resolve.

As well as the more cooperative ventures, and there is no doubt that jigsaws and constructional activities are most effective and enjoyable when children tackle them in twos and threes, competitive games such as *Snap* and *Happy Families* also have their place, particularly from the point of view of encouraging concentration and speed of response. Probably the best starting point for *Snap* cards is the simple representational material such as that to be found in the motifs on Christmas wrapping paper. This, suitably mounted and covered, is simple to prepare and sufficiently repetitive to build in a high possibility of successful calls. From this the children can progress to manufactured *Snap* games or to dominoes or to ordinary playing cards.

Commercially produced graded apparatus
At this stage it would be useful to give the children experience of manufactured graded apparatus in visual discrimination. The firm of Philip and Tacey provides a veritable mine of materials. Their range of apparatus is varied enough to give the children carefully graded practice

and experience in sorting and matching, acquisition of ideas of symmetry and reversal and of shape analysis. Many teachers rely exclusively on this material for their visual work. I feel that this is a mistake. Valuable though the material appears to be, it consists only of sets of graded cards and would be too difficult for many children unless they had prior experience in the direct handling and observation of a wide range of concrete materials in real situations. However, if the children have had such experience, the Discrim apparatus and the Hereward Observation Test and Matching Tablets can give valuable stimulation in visual discrimination and in the discerning of significant shape and spatial relationships. The Hereward materials are particularly demanding and it would appear to me inconceivable that a child who can handle these successfully would have difficulty in discriminating letter shapes and simple word patterns. Philograph Publications also produce a range of related exercises in shape matching, sorting and analysis in strip book form. Differentiation by colour reversal is also built in. These little books, the *Alike Unalike Strip Books*, are exceptionally tough. They have a spiral wire spine and will withstand most of the rough treatment one would expect of children inexperienced in handling books. The boxed apparatus called *Symmetry and Reversal Pairing Cards* gives valuable practice in discerning symmetrical relationships. The cards can also be paired off as complete reversals. This ingenious apparatus is exceptionally well childproofed and both sides of each card have a well-glazed surface which can be wiped clean in an instant with a damp rag. The *Shape Analysis Matching Cards* give graded practice in shape matching, reorientation skills and in the discerning of part–whole relationships.

Published readiness books

Not all children of school age require such detailed and comprehensive training in visual discrimination as has been outlined so far. However, with the expected growth in nursery education we shall be admitting into our schools children more chronologically immature than we have been accustomed to having. Also the provision of nursery places will be heaviest in places which were formerly designated educational priority areas. For these children the visual programme cannot be too comprehensive. There are also among the children of school age those who are mentally, socially, emotionally and physically immature for their age and their immaturity is likely to be reflected in poor visual abilities. For such children, treatment in addition to that already described will almost certainly be needed, and this can be provided by published readiness books. The best known and most comprehensive in scope are those published by Wheaton of Exeter as the readiness material for the *Happy Trio* reading scheme. There are three prereaders: *We read Pictures*, *We read more Pictures*, and *Before we read*. Each book contains forty-seven pages of varied prereading exercises. Page 48 gives page by page notes to the teacher and the inside back cover provides an index of the skills covered in the book. Though less comprehensive in coverage than the *Happy Trio* prereaders, *Getting Ready for Reading* (Books 1 and 2) published by Ginn as readiness material for the *Beacon* reading scheme, are very attractive. In addition to the teachers' notes on the inside back cover of each book there is a teachers' manual which gives detailed suggestions for the introduction and development of each page and for supporting activities. *Happy Trio* or *Getting Ready for Reading* can be used most advantageously if the teacher has the book and teaches it with groups small enough for each child to see it clearly and point to the items when asked. I would not recommend each child in the group having his own copy or sharing one with a neighbour. It is very difficult to control visual activity with a group of children unless the teacher can guarantee that all members of the group are focussing their attention on the point at issue at any one time. The teacher can best direct the activity by focussing attention on the one copy under her personal control.

A published, structured prelearning programme
For those not keen on improvising, or for those who lack storage or display space or have difficulty in effectively organizing a mass of discrete materials, there is on the market the highly structured 'learning to learn' kit, *Flying Start*, published by Holmes McDougall. This is the work of Dr D. H. Stott, designer of the well known *Programmed Reading Kit*. It consists of a variety of carefully graded puzzles, games and activities for both individual use and for playing in pairs. All the activities are self-correcting. Though providing sufficient materials to occupy up to forty children at any one time, the Kit is surprisingly compact and simple to organize. The cards are of uniform size, extremely durable and well finished and colour-coded for ease of distribution and collection by the children themselves. The whole kit takes up very little classroom space, especially if the specially designed PVC container is bought. This can be hung on the wall and in it any item can be readily located by teacher or children. When the container with the complete set of items in place is taken down for carrying, it can be folded to take up the space of an average shoe box. As the activities are designed progressively in sequence the teachers' manual is essential. One of the teacher's greatest problems in early learning is to systematically record and evaluate the very diverse experiences to which individual children are exposed. Teachers who use *Flying Start* find very helpful in this respect the structured individual

progress cards which can be ordered to accompany the kit. In order to prevent ordering 'blind' from the catalogue, and to avoid the possibility of buying a pig in a poke, the publishers make available to teachers centres and training institutions a twenty-two minute 16 mm film which demonstrates the *Flying Start* programme in use with reception class and preschool children. Lecturers experienced in the use of the kit are available in some areas to present the film, give advice and answer queries.

Distinguishing letter shapes

The ultimate test of the effectiveness of training in visual discrimination is the ability to sort and match accurately the letters of the alphabet, both capital and lower case forms. Most educational suppliers market sets of three-dimensional plastic letters and as these are easy to handle they should be used in the first stage of testing. Progression can then be made to cardboard letters which have little thickness and finally to print, minimum size 18 point.

Hand–eye coordination

Reading is rarely taught as reading only. It is (and should be) almost always accompanied by writing. They are sister skills and the one constantly reinforces the other. Skill in visual discrimination only will not produce writing. What is needed in addition is the ability to coordinate hand and eye effectively. The normal child starting school has sufficient powers of coordination to cope with the ordinary situations in which he finds himself. He can dress, wash and feed himself. To do the latter he demonstrates (as for example when transferring a spoonful of cornflakes from his dish to his mouth) a high degree of body awareness. He can accurately gauge both the distance and direction through which the spoon must be guided. He has a good idea of himself in relation to objects in space and can accurately control moving objects in space providing they do not move too quickly and are not too small. For example, he can catch a seven-inch ball with comparative ease if it is thrown to him over a distance of three yards, but would probably have a much lower success rate with a table tennis ball. Now when faced for the first time with writing he is confronted with the need to make extremely fine co-ordinations. The fairly massive body movements which have served him well so far are now no great help. If unguided he will write with his whole arm and complain of a sore shoulder after a time. The ability to make very finely controlled movements with fingers and wrists will only come to some children after a lengthy training involving a carefully planned progression of relevant experiences and activities. For many children, of course, much of this treatment will be unnecessary. The little girl whose mother has taught her to do simple sewing, knitting and embroidery, and is used to handling needles and to cutting out shapes with scissors has already had some useful manipulative experience before coming to school. Her brother has probably had similar experience with screws, nuts and bolts in his Meccano set and has probably helped daddy to hammer in nails and drive home screws. Both children have probably done some painting with small brushes and had crayons, Plasticine and pencil sets to occupy them on wet afternoons. The child who lacks such preschool manipulative experience must rely heavily on school enrichment programmes if he is to achieve competence in hand–eye coordination. Again it is recommended that the earliest experiences should be at a concrete level. Bead threading, manipulation of clay and Plasticine, sand and water play and activity with jigsaws, building blocks and constructional toys make good starting points. Progress can then be made to paper cutting, tracing, the use of templates and the colouring of the resultant shapes, and to drawing and painting. Published readiness books give numerous ideas for further exercises in motor coordination as, for example, when various outlines are first traced with the index finger and then with pencils on tracing paper.

Left–right eye movements

Mention has been made earlier in this chapter of the ability of the skilled reader to make smooth and rhythmical eye movements in a left to right direction followed at the end of each line of print by a backward and downward sweep to the beginning of the next line. Such ability does not come by accident. The small child, uninitiated in the conventions of print, can see no sense of order or direction in the confused mass of lines and squiggles that appear to make up the printed page. The four year old, when asked to copy adult writing or a page of the story book which mummy reads at bedtime, will gaily start at the bottom and work his way up to the top, and just as readily work from right to left as he will from left to right. The left-handed child is notoriously prone to writing in a right to left direction and who can blame him? This way he can at least see what he is doing without his hand getting in the way.

The *Happy Trio* and *Getting Ready for Reading* readiness books as well as parts of the *Flying Start* programme suggest numerous exercises for developing left to right eye movements. The 'path' technique is one example. Here the child is trained to trace with his index finger the route followed by a bee from flower to hive, by a bird from bird table to nest, by a train from tunnel to station, etc. Pictures which depict the episodes in sequence of nursery rhymes and of simple stories are also helpful. Here the children will point to the pictures as they repeat the relevant parts of the rhyme or as they listen to the teacher putting the story of the pictures into words. In all exercises involving visual discrimination, as when a 'foreigner' has to be identified in a set of otherwise similar elements, the teacher should seek to set good habits from the outset by training the child always to begin at the left and work towards the right as careful observation of each element is encouraged and the child is led to discover and note similarities as well as differences. Also, in memory training exercises, as related objects are added to the sequence, the additions should always be made at the right of the previous elements.

The teacher who favours phonic approaches will be aware that though the letters in words do not convey meaning as such, they do signal directions as to the type of sounds to be uttered and as to the sequence in which the sounds should be made. It appears to me that children who know their letters and are systematically taught to build new words in left to right sequences have great advantages over children whose exclusively look and say training gives them no word attack skills when faced with new vocabulary. In the latter case, because the beginner lacks the reading experience which enables him to make intelligent use of context, the only ploy available to him is to guess wildly. This explains the very common confusion between the words 'was' and 'saw'. In time, the majority of children get over this difficulty with increasing maturity. However, many such errors could be avoided, and much more sense made of early reading, if children had some phonic instruction.

Much more difficult to treat are those children who see 'was' as 'wsa' or as 'swa'. Such errors may be due to inadequate focussing ability and may indicate that the child has not achieved cerebral dominance. Whatever the reason, if children do make such errors with simple words it indicates that they have been put on formal reading too soon. For such children, more rather than less prereading activity is required.

Visual memory and imagery
Mention has been made in chapter two of the part played by memory, both long- and short-term, in reading. Recognition involves holding a mental image in the mind long enough to relate it to a similar image in the memory store. Children vary in the efficiency of their recall mechanisms. Most teachers will have had the frustrating experience of teaching certain children new words and reinforcing them with the repetition built into look and say primer pages and by additional work with flash cards, work books and teacher-devised activities, including tracing and copying, only to find that the next day the children have forgotten and approach the same words apparently for the first time. The usual reaction of the teacher is to grit her teeth and continue to administer the mixture as before. My

own opinion is that though there may be ultimate success, it is often only achieved as the result of such a dull and monotonous grind that there is little pleasure in such hard won achievement and that this practice induces negative attitudes towards reading from the very beginning. Children who have such difficulty are obviously not ready for formal reading and lack the perceptual and processing equipment essential to the task. Many teachers will also have had the experience of noting that a child will respond instantly and accurately to a word on a flash card and yet cannot recognize the word in context in print. Obviously the child is capable of forming a mental image but is relating it to associations, such as a tear or a thumbprint on the flash card itself, which are extraneous to reading. In such cases the chore of inefficient reinforcement procedures by apparently endless repetitions could be much reduced if attention were first paid to graded practice in forming and relating visual images of a more concrete kind. If experience in this area is inadequate, the children's power to retain and process perceptions of abstract symbols, which exactly mirror those in the print, is limited and this explains to some extent much of the wild guessing, omissions or substitutions which children make in early attempts at reading.

Training in visual memory is inseparable from all exercises in discrimination in which, in any series of objects or representations of objects, relationships involving 'same–different', 'bigger–smaller' etc have to be noted and discussed. To achieve success in any of these tasks an image has to be retained in the mind in order that the attributes of that image can be compared with other images in the series for sameness, difference, size order and the like. However, it is possible to concentrate more exclusively on the memorizing rather than on the matching and sorting elements by the use of certain exercises designed for that specific purpose. The commonest of these is the 'find the missing part' exercise. Here the child is presented with a picture of a table with three legs, a doll with one eye and other similar stimuli. He supplies the missing part by recalling visual images of tables, dolls etc from his actual experience of such phenomena and is led by observation and discussion to point out in what ways the object depicted is incomplete. Another common technique is the 'what's wrong here' or detection of absurdity exercise. Here the child is given pictures portraying items such as a house with the front door halfway up the wall, a jug with handle and spout on the same side or a car in motion with its driver in the back seat. The child compares the object presented with visual images recalled from memory of houses, jugs and cars within his experience in order to point out what is wrong. Many teachers omit the purely visual or pictorial stimulus in favour of verbal accounts. It would be beyond the powers of many children to detect the absurdity inherent in the spoken sentence 'The driver settled comfortably in the back seat, started up, and was soon speeding into the country'. Teachers should not be surprised at responses such as 'You shouldn't drive cars fast!' which show that the children have completely missed the point. The same children would have little difficulty if the stimulus were of a purely visual kind.

Teachers and children frequently enjoy the memory game in which the children are presented with a number of familiar objects on a tray. The tray is removed after a time and the children recall as many as possible of the elements in the original array. This activity is made much more useful as memory training and much closer to the type of memorizing important in reading if the children are encouraged to see the array, not as a number of discrete objects, but to scan it for relationships in which certain patterns can be discerned. For example, a comb, nail file, lipstick and purse could be separated from other objects as likely to be associated with the contents of a lady's handbag; needle, scissors, thimble as objects used in sewing form a different group from spoon, salt-cellar and sugar lump which are linked with the dining table. With such relationships as the basis, memorizing becomes a much more orderly and systematic process than the attempt to remember an apparently haphazard selection of objects.

An abundant provision of suitable pictures in which everyday objects and incidents are portrayed is necessary for training in visual memory and imagery. The children relate the pictures to retained mental images from their own experience, and the pictures form the stimuli by which the memory paths between the real world and the stored images by which it is represented and internalized are strengthened. The child will be unable to form such memory paths unless the visual material has been previously met in real situations. It is important therefore to start with pictures in which what is portrayed is familiar to the children. Philograph Publications produce a very good set called *Times through the Day* pictures. These are double-sided, very strong and treated with a wipe-clean surface. On one side are pictures of everyday scenes at home, e.g. getting-up, having breakfast; on the other side are school scenes such as playtime and 'doing our lessons'. Sets of smaller pictures, ideal for small group work, are the *People who work for Us* pictures produced by the same firm. More expensive, but certainly far more extensive than those already mentioned, are the admirable *Through the Rainbow Conversation Pictures* produced by Schofield and Sims. These pictures have their own built-in stand and are much easier to display and control than pictures which have to be mounted on the wall or held in the hand in order to be seen. As they fold into book form they are also easily put away and stored. There are also some excellent series of picture books on the market. However, as they are quite small compared with the pictures referred to above, it is essential for the teacher, not the children, to have the book and to teach it with groups small enough to see the pictures clearly. Some of the titles in the Ladybird series such as *Going to School, Shopping with Mother, Times through the Day* and *On the Farm* are excellent for training in visual memory and imagery as are all the Arnold's *New Colour Photo Books* and many of the titles in the Macdonald's *Starters* series.

As well as requiring the ability to recall isolated images and place them in a meaningful setting, reading also calls for the ability to recall and organize a succession of visual images in sequence. To remember the order of the letters in a syllable, the syllables in a word, words in a sentence, sentences in a paragraph and paragraphs in a story calls for great skill in accurately recalling abstractions for which considerable prior experience at a concrete and visual level seems necessary. For this, teachers rely a great deal on stories and nursery rhymes in which the main incidents are related in sequence in picture form. The children then recall the scenes orally and thus retell the story in sequence. Film strip and colour slide projectors are extremely useful in this respect for the presentation of material and I think it a pity that they are relatively so little used in nursery/infant schools. Perhaps the meagre requisition allowances available for the education of small children – one of the great injustices of our educational system – partly explains this. I also find it odd that the overhead projector is so little used with children at the infant stage. The possibilities of overhead projection for easy prepreparation, storage, retrieval and reuse of transparencies plus the facility with which material can be built up visually with the children participating, make it a much more flexible device for visual work than the blackboard, flannelgraph and other traditional resources.

Some teachers are extremely inventive in devising progressively graded activities in visual memory and imagery. However, for those less well endowed, or for inexperienced teachers or those without relevant training, the readiness books already described are very helpful.

Visual training and minority methods

The last decade or so has seen the introduction of a number of minority methods in the teaching of reading and some 10 per cent of the nation's children are being currently taught by innovations such as ita or by colour-cuing systems of which the most popular are Gattegno's *Words in Colour* and Jones's *Colour Story Reading*. Each of these approaches attempts, by different routes, to simplify some of the major difficulties and apparent inconsistencies inherent in our written language. ita attempts this by redesigning the characters of the traditional alphabet. In *Words in Colour* the language is broken down into its constituent sounds and each sound consistently identified with one of forty-one colours. *Colour Story Reading* uses three colours plus black in conjunction with three background shapes – square, triangle and circle. In each case there is ultimate transfer to traditional orthography with the various 'crutches' which characterize each approach removed. Though all children will not be equally ready to embark on any of the approaches described, there is little help for the teacher as to how she should prepare the children for the appropriate stage of perceptual readiness required to start on any one of them. Each of these approaches constitutes a relatively closed system, i.e. its structure and design limits the sort of help which the child learning to read by traditional methods can draw from the environment. To counteract this limitation and having in mind the necessity at transfer for adequate recognition of traditional orthography, it would seem appropriate and indeed necessary to give children who will later be introduced to formal reading via one of the minority methods at least the same provision in visual prereading skills which children who will begin on traditional approaches require.

A final note

In this chapter I have attempted for the benefit of students, teachers and others concerned with prereading, to break down into separate elements the visual skills which a child will need in order to make a successful start in formal reading. It is only by such compartmentalization that insights into those skills can be developed and appropriate techniques in skill teaching can be described and explored. However, and this theme will be constantly developed in subsequent chapters, the teaching of visual skills will rarely be done in isolation. For example, even if the teacher was concentrating specifically on visual discrimination, she would rarely exclude the opportunities for training in left–right orientation or in visual memory which might arise in a particular situation. Many of the teaching techniques described lend themselves to such diversification in skill development. Additionally, visual training is almost invariably accompanied by opportunities for simultaneously developing auditory, oral language and manipulative skills. Prereading is in fact a global process which aims at the fullest development of all those abilities which the child requires to make a good start in learning to read.

Chapter 4

Training in auditory skills

The visual aspects of reading and their importance in the process are fairly obvious to all students of the subject. This is an area which has been comparatively widely researched and, though not all the results are conclusive, certain elements have been identified as essential for success in reading and these form the basis of programmes in prereading visual training in which many teachers have some competence and experience, and for which most teachers recognize a need. Though teachers generally concede the importance of auditory factors as essential for success in beginning reading, these aspects are less widely researched than visual and oral language skills, and teachers are more unsure of what needs to be done in the field of auditory training and how to do it. A possible cause of the relative ignorance of auditory factors as determinants of reading success is that most people with any competence in reading habitually read silently and see no obvious link between hearing and the apparently unheard process of decoding print. If they were to stop and listen hard to themselves reading silently, they would be surprised to hear an inner voice repeating every word they read. Even the most experienced adult readers cannot refrain from subvocalization, i.e. it is impossible for them to dissociate the visual image evoked by the printed symbol from the sound image with which it corresponds. The fact that reading involves decoding, the translation of visually perceived symbols into sound, means that for every visual skill utilized in reading, a matching auditory skill is exercised. Thus visual discrimination of letter shapes and word patterns would not result in recognition without the corresponding ability to register auditorily the associated sounds. The left–right progression by which letters become visually linked as word patterns is matched to a time order of sound utterances which become sequential sound patterns. To be effective, visual memory requires a corresponding auditory memory. At the very beginning of formal reading, before he has developed fluency or skill in silent reading, the beginner reads aloud. It is only by hearing himself reading that he can prove to himself that he is reading at all.

Reading begins with perception. If the child cannot accurately perceive the sounds signalled by the letter and word shapes, he cannot begin to read. Poor auditory perception may be due to hearing defects or to delayed language growth. The latter may be caused indirectly by the poor quality of the language which he hears in the home. If the language heard is poorly enunciated, this may affect his ability to discriminate between certain sounds. Language growth may also be impaired by speech defects. The latter may be due to brain damage, respiratory difficulties, malformation and malfunctioning of the speech organs themselves, emotional problems (as with regression to baby talk or stammering), hearing defects and resultant weakness in auditory discrimination, and, of course, slow developmental pattern. If hearing or speech defects are severe, reading will not be possible. Some children are deaf in certain tonal ranges only and all children are likely to suffer temporary impairment of hearing if they have colds or catarrh. Children start school with auditory acuity only partially developed and this continues to grow throughout the period of schooling. Consequently the earlier children start school the greater is the need for careful consideration of the types of auditory work that may be undertaken and the purposes for which it may be done.

Recent research (Smythe *et al* 1972) supports the empirical evidence that there is a definite developmental trend with increasing improvement in phoneme discrimination ability at each successive year level, and that by the time children complete grade one they experience very few phoneme discrimination difficulties. However, we have to consider the relevance of research undertaken in Canada to our situation here in Britain, where our children start school one year earlier. The children referred to as having completed grade one would correspond to our top infants. Even these were shown to have some difficulties with consonant pairs v-th, f-th, and with m-n-g. My own experience is that many British five year olds have difficulty with the open vowel pair e-i, as in 'pet' and 'pit'; with the voiced-voiceless consonant pairs v-f, b-p, d-t, and with sh-ch as in 'shop' and 'chop'. A number of six year olds can still not discriminate accurately between r and w. They say, for example, 'wose' for 'rose' and confuse the r and w auditorily. When asked to associate the sounds signalled by the initial letters r and w to pictures, they assign the w to 'rabbit' (wabbit) and the r, which they confuse with w, to 'watch'.

In ordinary conversation such handicaps need not be crucial to understanding. The listener is aided by tone, emphasis, gesture, and the context of the speech. He is on the same wavelength as the speaker. In early reading there are few such props to accurate recognition and, as reading in context is not within the competence of the beginning reader, poor auditory perception results in inept errors which distort the meaning of the print and prevent comprehension.

46

The problem for the nursery/infant teacher is to evaluate the different auditory needs of the children in her class. She will be aware from her own observations and recording of pupil behaviour that some children have all the auditory equipment necessary for beginning reading. She must not assume, however, that all children are so equipped and she must be prepared, if necessary, to make available a wide range of graded auditory activity for those children who appear to need it. It is possible to test with some accuracy older children suspected of having auditory problems. With small children, testing is extraordinarily difficult. The accuracy of the tests depends to a large extent on the ability of the testee to understand the concepts on which the tester depends for his test construction and administration. Consider the type of informal test which teachers are (in my view, quite wrongly) advised to set to children suspected of poor auditory discrimination:

1 Listen to the *following* words. Which *sound* the *same* at the *end*?
   pig hat dig
2 Listen to these *words*. Which has a *different sound* at the *beginning*?
   hen leaf hat house
3 Listen to these *words*. Which one has a *different ending* from the others?
   coat boat train
4 Listen to these *words*. Which one *begins* with 'd'?
   bag dog pig
5 Listen to these *sounds*. What word do they make?
   c-a-t
6 Listen to these *words*. Which one has a *different sound* in the *middle*?
   cap hat cup van
7 Tell me some words that *begin* with 'j'.

The validity of such a test would depend largely on the ability of the testee to understand the auditory concept of the following terms: following, word, sound (noun), sound (verb), sounds (noun), sounds (verb), same, different, end, ending, begin, begins, beginning, middle. The tester also assumes understanding of the sounds associated with letter names. The research of Smythe and his associates reveals that hardly any five year olds had any understanding in an auditory context of 'sound' and 'word'; only 21 per cent understood 'letter name'; and only 25 per cent understood 'middle'. Other concepts and the percentage of children understanding them were measured as follows: 'same' (46 per cent); 'different' (54 per cent); 'end' (56 per cent); and 'beginning' (60 per cent). Six months later, and despite relevant instruction, only 2 per cent of the children had mastered the concept 'sound' and only 10 per cent the concept 'word'. It is obvious that with such tests, factors other than auditory discrimination are being measured and it is probable, therefore, that if any reliance is placed upon test results, exaggerated estimates of difficulty in auditory discrimination are likely to occur. The nursery/infant teacher's surest guide to evaluation of auditory difficulty is her own skilled observation and recording of errors. The same records will be equally useful as indicators of the readiness of children to profit from instruction in phonics.

In order to ensure that children get off to a good start in formal reading it is important for the teacher to be aware of the ways in which auditory ability affects reading success. She needs to know the auditory skills which are relevant to reading and how these may be developed so that she may remedy auditory deficiency where this is apparent and accurately assess the degree of readiness for formal reading which a given child may exhibit. In the first place, the child must accurately perceive the sound associated with the printed symbol. If the visual pattern c-a-t evokes the spoken response 'caravan', reading cannot be said to occur. The child has not achieved the understanding which is basic to reading that each word has its own distinctive sound pattern, and that the sound pattern can be analysed into a sequence of sounds which correspond to the left to right order of the letters.

Starting points in auditory work

The sounds associated with the letter shapes have no meaning in themselves. They are abstractions and in isolation are unrelated to anything within the small child's direct experience of the real world. Therefore, as with visual work, auditory training should begin at the child's level of experience. The first sounds to be introduced should be those with which the child is familiar in daily life. At the beginning, sounds should not be isolated from the objects, or representations of the objects, which produce them. There should be a visual clue with which the sound may be associated. Good pictures are a considerable aid to accurate auditory perception and discrimination and their value is enhanced if used in conjunction with a tape recorder. Following a farm visit a picture 'On the farm', with an accompanying tape recording of the sounds made by the different animals, sets up possibilities of much active, interesting work. The children listen to the sounds on tape and identify them by pointing to and naming the appropriate creatures on the picture. Names can also be given to the sounds themselves, e.g. lowing, purring, mewing, barking, neighing, bleating, braying, roaring and grunting. The auditory work thus stimulates vocabulary growth. On subsequent sessions the same picture can be used without the tape recorder and the children can be asked to imitate the noises associated with the various animals depicted. Later the tape recorder may be used without the picture and the children, by listening only, can be challenged to name the animal identified with each sound or to supply the correct names for the different sounds played. A zoo visit could stimulate similar tape and picture-based activities. A comprehensive range of all the common sounds associated with home, school and environment could be taught, given an intelligent collection of pictures and associated tape recordings.

In *Getting Ready for Reading*, Book 1, the pictures 'At home', 'On the farm', and 'At the seaside' are useful for small group work on the lines indicated above and the teacher's manual gives helpful suggestions for further development. Similar work can be based on pp. 25, 28 and 45 of *We read Pictures* and on pp. 1, 4, 38 and 45 of *We read more Pictures*.

The Language Master is a useful device which costs little more than a normal tape recorder. The teacher can prepare material on the blank cards provided for work with groups or individuals and can present simultaneously a picture and the sound associated with it. At later stages, letter shapes, words and sentences can be presented and synchronized with the appropriate sounds.

Still at the level of the children's actual experience, tape recordings of the voices of school staff saying merely 'Good morning, Miss Jones' (or whatever the teacher's name happens to be), give good opportunities for listening and identifying a series of sounds with a particular person. If all members of the school staff, including head, deputy, assistant teachers, caretaker, nursery nurses, secretary and canteen assistants, were taped, a good range of voices could be supplied. An obvious progression is to tape each child in the class making a similar greeting with the children taking turns to identify the speaker. Correct identification can be rewarded by having the speaker repeat the greeting personally. The same game can, of course, be played without a tape recorder by having the children take turns at being blindfolded and greeted by a speaker (one of the other children). The 'blind man' must name the speaker whose voice he hears. He is allowed up to three repetitions of the greeting. Children much enjoy an extension of this activity if they greet the 'blind man' in disguised voices.

For those not given to improvisation, or without the time or inclination to prepare material on the lines indicated above, the Remedial Supply Company produces two seven-inch hearing tapes which contain a good range of the sounds heard in real life situations.

Listening to words
Only when children have actual experience of the sounds made by creatures and objects in the real world, and have developed some competence in discriminating between them, will it be possible for them

to give meaning to the distinctive sound patterns by which we recognize words. A 'mountain' is merely an abstraction in sound to the small urban child who has never seen one. It becomes more meaningful as he gains direct experience, preferably by climbing one and by actually comparing one with others, as well as with hills, valleys and other contours, or by acquiring vicarious experience through pictures, film, television and the like. Until such experience is acquired, there is no possibility of forming a meaning-associated visual image and relating it to the distinctive sound pattern which those more linguistically competent would connect with the symbols m-o-u-n-t-a-i-n. While a sound pattern remains unrelated to a visual image, or may never have even been formed when the oral language background is deficient, recognition cannot take place. The visual stimulus, whether object, picture or printed word, evokes no response within the memory banks. There is no sound pattern there to be evoked. Children whose store of words is limited bark at print. They may be taught to perceive visually but cannot achieve recognition.

Many children from linguistically-impoverished homes owe much to school enrichment programmes for language growth. Teachers encourage language growth in a number of ways, not least by listening training. Most children have been used to listening almost since birth. They can hear before they can see and respond to spoken language long before they can focus visually with any clarity. However, the listening skills which the preschool child uses in normal situations are of a different kind from those involved in reading. To the child starting school the word 'bat' represents an object with which a ball is struck. A country child might also connect the word with a winged mouse which flits about in the evening. He would not normally be in a situation where the word needs to be considered in the context of its sound. If he were made to consider it in this light his response would probably be that the word (noise or thing) 'bat' says 'bat'. He could not conceive of its having three constituent sounds which form a pattern having a beginning, a middle and an end. It is also unlikely that he would see any relationship between 'bat', 'fat', and 'hat'. The listening training relevant to reading needs to be directed to very fine discriminations of a kind which are foreign to the young child's previous experience. The learner needs to detect very fine shades of sound difference and to discern relationships by which consistent sound patterns can be established. He must also relate those sound patterns consistently to abstract visual symbols, remember both in sequence and recall them accurately. Frequently he has to evaluate sound–symbol correspondences against other possible selections as when one letter which has a reversed equivalent with a different sound may not be in the immediate reading matter but may be evoked in the mind.

The three Rs of listening

Having named objects and associated them with certain sounds by exercises such as those suggested above, the child must then be trained to listen to words and sound patterns within words in order that differences and similarities may be detected and significant sound patterns may be perceived and retained within the memory. In order to do this, reliance is placed on the three Rs of listening – repetition, rhythm and rhyme. A wealth of repetition is built into the traditional stories told by teachers to small children. Not only are words, phrases and sequences repeated within the stories, but the stories themselves bear frequent retelling. The repetition inherent in small children's established favourites such as *The Three Bears* and *The Gingerbread Boy* is a great aid to memorization and as the children acquire confidence by familiarity, they take pleasure in anticipating the sequences and will supply the appropriate word or phrase if the teacher makes a challenging pause and encourages participation. Woe betide the teacher if she occasionally dares to vary a well-loved tale by presenting it in a novel way or alters the familiar delivery by so much as a single word. Her misdeed will be swiftly called in question by such reproachful comments as: 'You didn't say that last time, miss. You said . . .'. The earliest stories should be told with the pictures which illustrate them accompanying the oral presentation. Discussion and questioning directed at the fullest elucidation of meaning should accompany each pictorial sequence. As concentration and listening skill improve, the pictures may be withdrawn and emphasis placed on the auditory channel. After a time the children themselves retell the story with the aid of the pictures and, finally, from memory. Incidentally, *Getting Ready for Reading*, Book 2, contains helpful pictorial material for the story of *The Three Bears* and the accompanying teacher's manual has a number of suggestions for visuoauditory development based on this. The ideas are capable of adaptation to similar tales of simple sequential structure.

Similar work is done with nursery rhymes, which have the additional advantages of being short and self-contained. Memorization is helped by the accompanying rhythm and rhyme. Many teachers teach nursery rhymes purely by speech and neglect the prereading possibilities of accompanying visual material. In early auditory work we should always keep in mind the related skills of formal reading for which prereading is the preparation. Visual and auditory memory, imagery and sequencing need to go hand-in-hand. What is heard needs to be accompanied by what is seen. Nursery rhymes are ideal material for teaching left–right visual progression with the accompanying auditory sequencing which so closely models later reading. *Getting Ready for Reading*, Book 1, has an admirable sequence of nursery rhymes which accurately and progressively anticipates the process of early reading. Thus the story of Old Mother Hubbard is portrayed in two frames in which the simple details can be interpreted horizontally in two fixations from left to right. *Humpty Dumpty* extends the eye movements by an additional horizontal, left to right frame. *Little Miss Muffet* is portrayed in two pairs of frames, one pair above the other. From the right-hand frame of the top pair the eye has to move to the left-hand frame of the bottom pair, thus practising on pictorial material the backward and downward sweep necessary in later reading at the end of each line of print. These eye movements are later reinforced by similar treatment of *Hey, Diddle, Diddle* and, in Book 2, of *The Queen of Hearts*. The illustrations are clear and simple, and so arranged as to suit ideally the oral phrasing and retelling of the stories concerned. Though the material is sound, there are disadvantages in presenting it in book form. The teacher has to make sure that each child is at the right place in the book and that each is pursuing the right activity at the right time. To ensure that teacher and children are in step, the groups being taught at any one time must be very small indeed. The ideas could be put across much better and to much larger groups of children if the material, instead of being in book form, was blown up to classroom chart size, say 20″ × 30″. With large pictures the teacher can more easily control both the teaching material itself and the focussing of the children's attention upon it.

Group games and activities
Allied to nursery rhymes and equally useful because of the inherent repetition and accompanying rhyme and rhythm are the various singing games and activities such as 'Poor Mary sits A-Weeping', 'Here we go round the Mulberry Bush' and 'Ring O'Roses'. These are not usually associated with visual stimuli as the accompanying movements and activities are self-explanatory. The sung number games such as 'Once I caught a Fish Alive', 'I saw Three Ships', 'Three Blind Mice', 'Ten Green Bottles' and 'The Twelve Days of Christmas' are also helpful for teaching important number words and concepts, while the visual aspects can be simply portrayed by flannelgraph.

It is possible through such games to extend the listening work to the hearing and identification of different rhythms. The teacher taps out the underlying rhythms of the singing games within the children's repertoire and challenges the children to identify them. The children join in and tap out the rhythm as they join in the songs. This activity is extended later to work with percussion and musical instruments.

Games such as 'Simon says' also help to encourage listening and reacting to oral instructions in an active way.

Phoneme discrimination

The phonemes are the basic sounds of our language and they can be represented in some 2,500 combinations to produce all the words of English. Opinions vary as to how many separate phonemes there are. This depends partly on whether one includes the consonants c, q or x in one's list. C has no phonemic value of its own. It is sounded as k except when followed by e or i, when it takes the sound s. Qu can be formed by blending the sounds associated with kw and x by ks. Opinions also vary about the sound that 'ng' makes in words like 'singing'. In ita it was found necessary to include a separate character to distinguish the particular sound from that associated with n – contrast the n in 'sin' with that in 'sing'. Consequently, a list of phonemes is a somewhat arbitrary matter and the number listed may vary between forty-one and forty-five.

For the purposes of phoneme discrimination the following list of forty-two seems comprehensive enough:

Short vowels
    a as in h*a*t
    e as in h*e*n
    i as in p*i*n
    o as in h*o*t
    u as in c*u*p
    oo as in b*oo*k

Long vowels
    ay as in d*ay*
    ee as in s*ee*
    ie as in p*ie*
    oe as in n*o*
    oy as in b*oy*
    ew as in f*ew*
    oo as in m*oo*n
    ow as in c*ow*

Extended vowels
    ar as in c*ar*
    air as in h*air*
    or as in n*or*th
    er as in f*er*n

Consonants
    b as in *b*ed
    d as in *d*og
    f as in *f*og
    g as in *g*ate
    h as in *h*at
    j as in *j*am
    k as in *k*itten
    l as in *l*eaf
    m as in *m*an
    n as in *n*et
    p as in *p*ig
    r as in *r*ed
    s as in *s*un
    t as in *t*ap
    v as in *v*an
    w as in *w*all
    y as in *y*ellow
    z as in *z*oo
    th as in *th*umb
    th as in *th*is
    sh as in *sh*oe
    ch as in *ch*air
    zh as in televi*s*ion
    ng as in si*ng*

In addition there is the schwa, the indeterminate vowel, which is represented by the letters italicized in the following words: the, arrive, doctor.

It would seem reasonable in any scheme of auditory training to familiarize the children with all the basic sounds they are likely to meet when later they come to reading. However, I know of no commercially-produced prereading programme sufficiently comprehensive or systematic to ensure that the children are not only acquainted with all the phonemes but also given graded practice in discriminating between them. We cannot assume that the preschool language experience of all children encompasses the total range of phonemic distribution. For the silent, withdrawn child, the child whose parents rarely speak to each other or to him, the child who has been in hospital for long periods or has spent much of his infancy in institutions – for such children, treatment far more systematic than we have been accustomed to giving is probably necessary. We must, too, bear in mind the limited auditory experience and acuity of the chronologically immature children for whom our rapidly growing nursery classes and schools have to cater. Surely for these children there will be time and opportunity for more than the unstructured play and socialization which has occupied the nursery day for so long? Cannot some systematic prereading teaching be done by nursery/infant teachers systematically trained to do it? Teaching of this order is currently handicapped by the dearth of well-organized and programmed materials, particularly in the auditory field. The readiness books in common use give far less attention to phoneme discrimination than they do to visual factors. There are many omissions in the so-called listening sections and the items selected lack systematic structure and development. Another impediment to auditory training is the current overemphasis on look and say teaching with the overworked flashcard as the main teaching resource. At least the teacher who is sensitive to the need for phonic work will attempt to teach the children their letters and thereby give some attention to important auditory factors. However, as a glance at the phoneme list above will indicate, much more than the letters of the alphabet has to be attempted and in ways much more thorough and systematic than are currently fashionable. Few infant schools avail themselves of the excellent material in the early stages of Stott's *Programmed Reading Kit*, produced by Holmes McDougall. The *giant touch cards*, properly handled, teach the correct phonic sounds of all the letters (lower case only) of the alphabet, plus those associated with the consonant digraphs ch, sh and th, in an active, interesting way. The cards are big enough for the whole class to be taught as one. When not being used for direct teaching they can form a good alphabet frieze to which the children can refer for handwriting practice or when playing games such as 'I Spy'. Work with the giant touch cards is then reinforced with sets of the small pupils' touch cards with which the children play in pairs or small groups in enjoyable activities such as the frame game. The activities are entirely self-correcting and there is little need of teacher intervention or support. The letter sound concepts learned from the touch cards are then extended to the *first letter cards* for self-correcting activity, again in pairs or small groups. The first letter bingo games provide opportunities to bring the whole class together to consolidate the work in an enjoyable, mildly competitive activity under the teacher's direction. With practice in this activity, after a time children who are a little ahead of the rest can take over from the teacher to be in charge of selected groups. As with the *Flying Start* materials already mentioned, the teacher's manual is essential for effective use of the items in Stott's *Programmed Reading Kit*. One advantage of the kit, unlike *Flying Start* which has to be ordered *in toto*, is that the manual and each item may be purchased separately. This is helpful to the teacher who is only concerned with prereading, as she need only order the four items mentioned. I might add that all the Stott materials are extremely tough and reasonably childproof. The publishers provide film/lecture facilities free to interested bodies. The film *Johnny can learn to read* runs thirty-one minutes.

Practical teaching of auditory factors associated with teaching the letters will be considered in some detail in chapter 7.

References

SMYTHE, P. C., STENNETT, R. G., HARDY, M. and WILSON, H. R. (1972) Developmental patterns in elemental reading skills: phoneme discrimination *Alberta Journal of Educational Research* 18

Chapter 5

Oral language development

The need for a very wide range of prereading activities is evident when one surveys the varied backgrounds and abilities of the thirty or so children who make up the typical reception class. Their backgrounds will vary from the (educationally) good home, full of books (many of which will have been read to the children by their parents), to backgrounds where the one book in the house is used to stand the teapot on. Varying social and cultural backgrounds will result in some children having speech adequate to their needs and some whose speech is little more than a grunt, or at best a monosyllable. Some will be confident, widely travelled, with a useful fund of experiences and working concepts at their finger tips. Such children are ready for anything and to them the new world of school is challenging and exciting. Others appear to be barely loosed from their mother's apron strings and, if we allow it, will cope with school by withdrawing from it and retreating, right at the very beginning, into an apparent dullness which may well prove invincible. Some, once they are accustomed to the new environment of school, will be ready to read very soon, while there are even the odd ones who can already perform this miracle before they come. Others will need time, some a great deal, for the school to provide the enrichment and the experiences which many a home is incapable of giving. No aspect of prereading is more crucial than that of oral language development. The greatest challenge to the reception class teacher is how to reproduce in a classroom for thirty or more children, given only five hours a day for two hundred days at most, a rich language environment that more fortunate children have enjoyed during their first five years.

There are many who doubt whether schools, especially those in down-town areas, can hope to set up the language equipment of the middle-class home and point to the apparent failure of the Headstart programme in the United States and of other such compensatory ventures. However, if our schools do not provide enrichment, who will? We at least know what our major problem in a prereading programme is. It is the need to provide opportunities for speaking and listening on many topics with other children and adults, and especially with the teacher herself. It is through speech, the major means of communication, that ideas and concepts grow, so that when reading starts, words have meaning. The words to be read have been met first in speech and the objects and concepts met in books have been experienced in real-life situations before they are met in print.

Schools can bring to bear a number of important factors for positive development of the language and vocabulary growth of small children. The first of these is the teacher herself. The use to which the teacher puts language, the attitudes, ideals and expectations of the teacher reflected in her own language, her power to motivate by positive handling of the experiences to which she exposes the children, these factors make her a much more powerful influence in language development than the peer groups to which a child may belong. The interest and role patterns of such groups are often ephemeral and because of their immaturity the language of the members is restricted. The teacher, who is herself not a member of such groups but whose position, above and beyond them, gives her the vantage point of all-seeing observer, is uniquely well placed to identify the isolated in her class and by sensitive handling to integrate them into appropriate social intercourse and activity. She is considerably helped in her language tasks by the child-centredness of current school climates. In the not too distant past, when children were expected to be seen and not heard and to sit still and listen, there is little doubt that what was written or read was overemphasized and that speech was firmly discouraged.

Nowadays, there is almost universal recognition of the need for the fullest encouragement of oral activity, not only in quantity but also in quality. Where quality is concerned, our most pressing needs are to make children sensitive to situations when speaking or listening must be judged to be the more appropriate, to the kinds of speech suitable to different occasions and situations, and to help them to acquire some sensitivity to standards. In all this the children have a constant model – their teacher. She too, today, will be less concerned with the number of facts which her children learn than with the ways in which they learn them. She will see herself as much less a full-time instructor than as a social engineer whose major function is the organization of experiences and activities (not least oral activities) from which learning may grow. To enable her to do this the formal settings of the past where vast numbers of children sat in serried ranks, silent and immobile as the very furniture itself, have been replaced by more informal classroom arrangements. The numbers of children to be handled, though still excessive when one considers all that has to be done, are also more generally manageable than they have been. There is additional help, though it is still far from adequate, from classroom aides, infant helps and school meals supervisors, which relieves her of some of her nonteaching chores. There is every need for such help if the teacher is to foster a suitable climate for language growth. Basic to such a climate is the permissive atmosphere in which the child grows by his own active participation. To provide the enriched background which is necessary needs sensitive awareness of the changing needs and interests of the children which demands constant planning and thinking ahead. To motivate all the children positively needs an appreciation of a wide range of individual differences so that individual goals may be clearly conceived and suitable programmes may be formulated to achieve them.

In chapter 4 I touched on some of the ways in which oral language is developed. There I was more concerned with the listening aspects of language. Now I wish to return to these and to look at them in more detail with the accent more on the speaking than on the listening end.

Direct speech experience

Language grows best when it arises naturally from activities and situations which are full of meaning and interest for children. The more attractive the activity, the more the children will want to participate. Withdrawal is most likely to result from activities which the children consider dull and uninteresting. However, it is not enough merely to organize appropriate experiences and leave the children to them. The possibility of language growth must not be left to chance. Rather, when planning this or that experience, the teacher must also include in her planning the fullest exploitation of those factors which promote the growth of vocabulary and ideas, and the structure in which those ideas may best be communicated to others. She will do this most economically by whole-class teaching and particularly by appropriate questioning and other teacher-directed follow-up activity.

Excursions

Excursions within the immediate environment of the school can generate fruitful opportunities for direct speech. This can occur en passant as the children discuss informally with their partners the sights and sounds which are met on the way. The learning will be more effective if the children are led to look, listen and remember by the expectation of exercises which the teacher is certain to initiate immediately on return. The immediate environment can be exploited most profitably by quite brief walks of a few hundred yards. These need to be planned so that each walk has a limited, clearly defined goal – the close observation of one aspect only of the environment. One morning, for example, the walk might focus on the shops, on their names, the goods sold or displayed, the activities observed, and the sounds heard. On return, the children can play a variation of the game 'We went to market and we bought . . .', adapted to 'We walked past the shops and we saw . . .'. The teacher might start off the game with 'I went past the greengrocer's and I saw some apples'. The children then take turns to repeat what has been said before and to add an item of their own. Thus the first child could say, 'I went past the greengrocer's and I saw some apples and some oranges'. When the children's memories become heavily taxed by the number of items in the list, the teacher can change the setting and initiate a different set of items, such as 'I went past the *butcher's* and I saw . . .'. If in the first round the emphasis is on listing nouns, a second round could be devoted to verbs, for example 'I went past the butcher's and he was cutting meat'. A third round could focus on sounds heard, for example 'I went past the butcher's and I heard him sharpening his knife'. In addition to the participatory activities described, good questioning on the part of the teacher can revise and consolidate new vocabulary and encourage self-expression so that simple ideas can be conveyed in clear short sentences. She should attempt to include all the children in the questioning by pausing after each question, so that all the children have time to think and respond. In questioning sessions the withdrawn child should be encouraged to greater productivity by opportunities to repeat simple sentences arising from the teacher's questions, for example:

'What did you see at the greengrocer's?'
No answer.
'Well, you saw apples, oranges and bananas?'
'Yes.'
'Well then, you tell me about them. You went past the greengrocer's and you saw apples, oranges and bananas. Now you tell me.'
'I went past the greengrocer's and I saw apples, oranges and bananas.'

Given simple activities and questioning of the types suggested above, short walks within the neighbourhood of the school could be devoted to the different jobs and occupations noted; the weather; the creatures seen; the types of houses; different styles and items of clothing; colours; public buildings, e.g. museum, library, art gallery, Town Hall, police station, fire station, hospital, railway station; different forms of transport; roadworks and building sites; the park. A nearby park can be visited time and time again to observe tree and flower displays at different times of the year, and can provide treats such as joining in activities in the children's play area, feeding the ducks or having an occasional paddle in the paddling pool.

Occasionally, longer excursions farther afield may be planned, for example to the zoo, to a farm, or to the seaside. No amount of pictures, however good, can ever make the impact which rivals the feeling 'I was there. I saw these things myself. I heard them, smelt them, touched them. I compared one real thing with another. I was a part of the zoo, the farm, the seaside that day. I lived it.'

Constructional activities

Almost all children like to make things. It gives a sense of pride and achievement when a child can say, 'Look, I made that myself.' At first, small children like to make things by themselves. They do not mind other children being about but cannot bring themselves to join in with others. At this stage they are keen to explore their own powers and need opportunities to practise and consolidate new skills. Though children at this egocentric stage of growth will frequently talk to themselves about their particular tasks, such language is not so important as communication with others. To make such communicative language possible, many children need positive training in cooperation. They must be taught to be patient, to wait for others, to take their turn. They learn these things best at first by playing in pairs and in this respect many teachers find most useful the *Merry-Go-Rounds* in the *Flying Start* materials. Once they can work with others, constructional activities give rise to many opportunities for functional language. There is a need to discuss what shall be made, how, with what and for what purpose. As problems arise during the actual construction these must be talked over as possible solutions are attempted. There is great scope, too, when the job is finished for the teacher to encourage the builders to talk about their models with the other children. Nowadays there is a great deal of constructional material which children find attractive. There are blocks of all kinds and sizes which can be made into trains, planes, cars, buildings, and furniture. Many of these large block materials can occupy quite large groups of children on a common task. For working in pairs or small groups there is Bildit, Junior Meccano and, most popular and least messy of all, Lego, which is just as popular with girls as with boys. In addition to commercially-produced constructional materials there is wood which many of today's teachers encourage small children to exploit with hammers, nails and saws. Waste materials such as cardboard boxes, toilet roll centres and plastic containers of all kinds are also used and much language arises naturally as ways and means of transforming these into the desired model are discussed.

Imaginative play
The Wendy house and the dressing-up box put the children in role-playing situations in which they need to use language appropriate to their

role. A great deal of functional language grows naturally out of Wendy house activities such as organizing a tea party, making the beds, using the phone and clearing away. Similarly, by selecting from the dressing-up box certain props, the child not only takes on the outward trappings of a role, he also assumes the character and language of the character portrayed. Thus the children, especially if encouraged to dress up in pairs, can adopt interchangeable roles of cops and robbers, doctor and patient, king and queen, and the like. Thus quite naturally, and without teacher intervention or direction, the need to use language and to harness it to purposes beyond ordinary, everyday usage grows spontaneously from simple starting points.

Mime, drama and movement
It is a short step from the spontaneous role-playing described above to teacher-directed activity exploiting the possibilities of mime and drama. Mime encourages closer observation and discussion of the simple activities and situations of daily life. At first, the teacher will concentrate on actions only, seeking to rectify ineptitude and lack of detail in the actions themselves. She will do this not only by demonstrating correct movements physically but by verbalizing explanations as well. As the children copy her and gain expertise, the obvious development is for them to verbalize their actions too. If the children mime individually or in small groups, the rest of the class should be encouraged to observe performances critically and put forward suggestions for improving performance. Those with suggestions to put forward should be invited to contribute both by deed and by word. In this way, audiences need not be mere passive onlookers but are likely to become as much involved with the activity and its resulting language as the performers themselves. Similar opportunities for critical discussion and participation occur in movement, PE and games.

Like mime and movement, unscripted drama is an activity which children enjoy. It can be used to promote pupil participation in nursery rhymes for sheer fun as well as being a great aid to comprehension of the vocabulary and concepts presented by the teacher through stories.

The daily life of the school
The minutiae of the school's daily round, allied with the current philosophy which increasingly fosters cooperative and participatory learning ventures, result in an almost unlimited variety of situations which encourage growth in oral language. Almost all infant classes have a daily news period during which the children are free to contribute items of interest. These may be personal, stemming from some happening in school, at home, or in the immediate environment and if there are many

children wishing to have a say, entire news periods may be taken up with children's contributions. At other times, the teacher may provide the starting point by raising issues of common interest. These may range from the purely local, e.g. discussion of some future class visit, to matters of international interest such as a moon-landing or a walk in space. However, the more the news is the children's own, the greater its interest and impact. If occasionally contributions appear to be flagging, it may be insufficient to stimulate discussion of television programmes, pets, birthdays, weather charts, news of sick classmates in hospital and the like, most of which stem from outside school. If all the talk centres on home, teachers should seriously question the experiences provided in school. It may be that the children do not find these sufficiently interesting to be worth talking about.

School assembly used to be almost entirely teacher-dominated. Nowadays it would be unusual for children not to make considerable contributions to acts of corporate worship, to which parents, too, are frequently invited. The children see some point not only in discussing and organizing their contributions but also in rehearsing in order to give their presentations a suitable polish.

Discovery methods and the need to work in groups result in much discussion of ways and means and the need to report findings and share them with others who may be working at different levels in different areas. Simple projects which involve the breaking down of some common theme or starting point lead to diverse strands of work which need to be tied together as the project approaches fruition. The children relate their findings and tell of work done or in hand, so that all may contribute to the pool of knowledge and achievement. Lacking as yet the ability to express thoughts in writing, the children are encouraged to communicate by drawing, painting, colouring, modelling and similar forms of creative expression. In such activities the teacher has constant opportunities through language of refining concepts of shape, size, colour, position, direction and function. Individual children should be encouraged to describe the pictures and objects they have made.

The richer the stimulation of the classroom environment, the more the children will want to talk about the objects and activities which interest and excite them. Colour tables, nature tables, interest and discovery tables, friezes, models and displays of work give much to talk about. Exhibitions should be mounted attractively and changed frequently in order to keep pace with the changing seasons and the widening knowledge and range of interests of the children. Picture books, well displayed and freely accessible to children, also give opportunities to 'read the pictures' and discuss them informally with friends. If the classroom is attractive and well organized, the children take pride in the things around them and need little encouragement to escort visitors on a guided tour of their treasure house, pointing out items of interest and giving explanations on the way.

All through the day incidental opportunities arise for the children to hear, use and respond to language. A great deal of teacher activity is taken up with giving instructions. Today's children seem to have great difficulty in following even the clearest and simplest oral directions. Where this is so, teachers would be well advised to give more than merely incidental training but to formalize this directly by activities such as 'Simon Says'. The more withdrawn children can be encouraged to greater verbal productivity by being made responsible for transmitting and receiving many of the messages which are necessary in the day to day running of the school. In some schools children take turns on telephone duty, answering incoming calls and transmitting messages to the head or school secretary and occasionally making outgoing calls under the head's direction.

Some schools form experience exchange links with other schools in the neighbourhood. Interesting activities and the children's accompanying commentaries and explanations are put on tapes or cassettes which are interchanged with those of the schools associated with the project.

Indirect speech experience

Not all speech experience in school can be acquired directly by first-hand acquaintance with actual stimuli or in real-life situations. Fortunately, today's schools have available to them a wealth of pictorial material which makes possible vicarious experience of objects and ideas which children would not come into contact with otherwise. Such experience is enhanced by a growing technology, embracing radio, television, the tape recorder, filmstrip and film projector, record player and slide projector.

Good, big pictures provide a focus on which the attention of the whole class can be fixed. They are invaluable for introducing new ideas as well as for revising concepts already met. Most teachers rely heavily on pictures to teach new vocabulary. The first stage is to get the children to name the various objects depicted. With new vocabulary a certain amount of repetition will usually be necessary. The slower children, or those with a tendency towards withdrawal, need several opportunities to hear, say and learn each new word. They should be encouraged to attend and to participate by repeated questioning, e.g. What is this? What is its name? What is it called? The teacher should pronounce the name distinctly and call on several members of the class to repeat the name in turn. One-word answers should be discouraged. 'It's a . . .', or 'This is a . . .', or 'It is called a . . .' are preferable as the children learn the rhythms and patterns of clear structured sentences.

The naming stage should be followed by work in classifying the objects learned into appropriate groupings. At first, classification will be decided on the basis of the more concrete or visual characteristics such as size, shape, texture, colour or number. In time, more abstract bases for classification, such as purpose or origin, should be sought. In order to accomplish this they must be encouraged to verbalize likenesses and differences. At first it is easier to spot and verbalize differences and the earliest differences will probably have as their basis some obvious physical characteristic, such as colour or shape. For example, the children are looking at toys of different kinds. The children may observe that the Lego piece is small or red and white, while the bicycle is big and is blue. A less obvious (and therefore higher order) difference is that though both are toys, one is used in the house and the other in the street. In dealing with likenesses, again higher order relationships should be encouraged. Young children may observe that a cat and a dog are alike because they each have four legs. A more abstract relationship is that both are animals. This is a higher order response in that familiar objects have been regrouped into a new class, which is itself capable of a new grouping, say, in this case, 'quadruped'.

Pictures are also a considerable aid to descriptive activity. It is much easier to describe with the stimulus of a picture than from memory alone. Much imaginative training can also be given if pictures are used as the starting point of stories which the children develop in their own words. The different outcomes which result can then be discussed for suitability, credibility or popularity. Pictures can also stimulate memory training as children observe details closely and then, either with pictures withdrawn or with eyes closed, verbalize what they 'see'.

Spoken language activities

Stories

Teachers lay great stress on certain spoken language activities which they themselves initiate, organize and direct. Of these, the most widely used are stories, nursery rhymes and poetry. Though enjoyment should be the keynote of all such activities, teachers are aware that properly handled these are important means of developing vocabulary, listening power and anticipatory and imaginative skills. Television and radio can present such activities extremely well with supporting material such as sound effects and music for good measure. However, broadcast material may be transmitted at inconvenient times, and even when the timing is suitable, the programme content may not be. Here the teacher scores over the communications industry in no small way. She can time her story for the precise moment when she feels her children are ready for it. She can select, present, and pace her material to suit the needs of her own particular class. The teacher-told story is special, intimate and personal, and extremely flexible. It can revise facts and situations arising from previous work, reinforce and consolidate work in hand, lead to new interests or expand existing ones. It can be didactic, sheer fun, thought-provoking or therapeutic. It can be as long or as short as the teacher chooses to make it and almost every part can be put to direct teaching use, especially through questioning, because the teacher controls it all the way. Questioning is essential in the first place in order to command and maintain attention. Many of today's children have poor listening skills. They appear to be listening yet can be miles away. They soon learn that some teachers are easily deceived by expressions of rapt attention. They are safe in the knowledge that the teacher will not question them or that they will be passed over if they are slow in responding.

Obviously stories should not be continually broken up by a constant barrage of teacher's questions so that the whole thing becomes a punitive operation. Questioning is certainly necessary before the story begins to prepare the children for the appropriate mental set, to tune them in so that they are not wildly floundering in uncharted territory, and to heighten pleasurable feelings of expectancy. As new vocabulary and concepts are introduced, questioning is necessary to ensure full understanding. The same questions should be asked several times in every part of the class. Children should also be encouraged to question the responses of others. Questions should not be aimed entirely at a level of basic vocabulary and literal comprehension. At climactic moments questioning should encourage critical thinking and prediction of likeliest outcomes. During a suitable pause, questions such as 'What do you think is going to happen now?' challenge the children to pit their wits against the author. If several outcomes are hypothesized, further discussion can be generated by such questions as 'Now, why do you think that?'. Such questions encourage reasoning and lead naturally to further discussion if the teacher then seeks evidence from the story by asking, 'What did I read to make you say that?'. Children should also be encouraged to verbalize their own personal experiences when they approximate to those in the story. Such observations heighten interest and involvement and encourage identification with the characters and incidents described. By questioning techniques such as these the whole class is stretched throughout the story to a high level of excitement and verbal activity.

Students in training and inexperienced teachers frequently fail to extract from their story-work the maximum possible feedback. This may result from inadequate preparation and the feeling that the story is a soft option. Insufficient attention is given to the actual selection of material and the purposes for which the story is to be told. Often the only apparent purpose is to settle the children down at the end of a long day and to gather them conveniently together prior to putting their coats on ready for an orderly dismissal. Occasionally this may be a valid exercise, but if such an attitude persists, many valuable opportunities for language development will be missed. Such attitudes result in extreme passivity on the part of the children and will not accomplish the major goal of prereading – motivating the children to want to read for themselves. The story should be as well prepared as any other lesson. Ideally it should be told, not read. This should involve the summarization of the main stages and its paraphrase by the student into lively, contemporary language. You can't tell what you don't know. Secondly, the actual delivery and presentation should be rehearsed. Students are often appalled when they hear tape recordings of their stories. They should tape the story before it is told to the children as part of their lesson preparation. As they listen to themselves they should note defects in presentation. The commonest of these are too rapid pacing, monotonous delivery and poor enunciation and these can be overcome given the will and a tape recorder. Without such practice, the weaker students pitch into the story and gallop along without ever taking their eyes from the book. It takes a great deal of time and practice to develop the eye–voice span of the experienced teacher who can read from the book with hardly a glance at the printed text. Lacking such expertise the neophyte should work at presentation the hard way. If all your attention is on the print you will soon lose the attention of the children.

Defining purposes, selecting material and rehearsing presentation are not enough to guarantee a successful story session. Important questions must be prepared in language which the children can understand. Attention will have to be paid to questions which introduce the children to the beginnings of the story and relate their own experience to it. It may be that an appropriate picture could be introduced at this stage. New vocabulary and concepts may need to be elucidated. Questions should be prepared with this in mind and timed for the most appropriate moments. More challenging open-ended questions leading to critical thinking and anticipation should be prepared at suitable stages. All questions should be written down as part of lesson preparation.

However, even where thorough questioning is documented as part of prelesson preparation, students frequently fail to capitalize on feedback potential through ignorance of the mechanics of actual questioning when the story is under way. Too often they accept the first response offered and unconsciously restrict their questioning to the most responsive group. The story degenerates into a dialogue between the teacher and one tiny section of the class. Other sections are thus encouraged to be apathetic or disruptive. When a question is asked it should be followed by a pause long enough for the teacher to include all sections of the class within her questioning gaze. The gaze should be a silent invitation for *all* children to react to the question. The pause guarantees the time for the children to think about it. When a majority of children signify (possibly by raised hands) a willingness to respond, the teacher should spray the question repeatedly at different ability levels. Different children should then be encouraged to discuss the responses of other individuals, while those with a tendency to opt out should be brought into action by being asked to repeat something previously stated or to make some comment or observation of their own. Only thus can the whole class be kept at a high level of activity and involvement.

Inept questions frequently result in 'Yes' or 'No' answers. These should be rephrased to guarantee reflective responses. The aim of questioning is to encourage children to think. The possibility of one-word answers should be guarded against on the lines indicated on page 59. Not only do we want the children to think, we also want them to verbalize their thinking and to communicate it with the appropriate rhythm, pattern and structure of short, lucid sentences.

Incidentally, there are innumerable occasions when questions are asked for information only. Here it pays to frame the question in such a way that the information required, and nothing else, is elicited. Consider the babel of confusion and disruptiveness that could be generated by the question, 'Have you all got pencils?'. Simultaneously a number of children will be saying 'Yes', a number saying 'No', and individual responses such as 'I have two', 'Miss, Johnny's pinched mine', 'Miss, I'm sharing with Mary'. Presumably the only point of the question was to determine who did *not* have a pencil in order that they might then be provided with one. In such cases, questions should be phrased as instructions, for example 'Put up your hand please if you have *not* got a pencil'.

Stories and questioning on stories most powerfully involve the pre-reader in experiences akin to those which he will meet when later he can read for himself. If stories are enjoyed the children may feel the need from time to time to mime them, dramatize them, retell them in their own words, or recreate the experience gained in drawing, painting, modelling and the like. In all such follow-up activities the teacher should capitalize on the opportunities for talk which arise.

Nursery rhymes and other verse
Nursery rhymes are meant to be enjoyed, but this should not prevent teachers from exploiting their enormous potential for language teaching. Many children will be familiar with a large number of rhymes. They will

have listened and watched with mother to radio and television programmes for the preschool child in which nursery rhymes are a constant feature. After the programme, many will have mimed and acted out the rhyme presented and in time many children acquire an extensive repertoire. A nursery rhyme sing-song is a common feature at bathtime or bedtime in homes where parents find time to devote to their children. Unfortunately when both parents are at work or otherwise prevented from giving the child the time and attention which is his due, there is no opportunity to hear and enjoy nursery rhymes. The school, therefore, must provide the opportunities.

As a teaching medium, nursery rhymes are extremely versatile. They come in all sizes from very short and simple to quite long and complex. They can be spoken or sung, acted or mimed. Through them the child is introduced to new vocabulary and language patterns. Rhyme is an aid both to anticipation and memorization, while the strong rhythms reinforce the basic structures of our language. They are a great aid to development of concepts of 'alike', 'different' and 'opposite' and therefore to categorization. Many rhymes are sheer nonsense and thus provide the earliest opportunities for detecting incongruities and absurdities in oral language. This is perhaps the first step towards critical thinking.

Because nursery rhymes are short they can be slotted in at almost any time in the school day. There are inevitable 'natural breaks' in the daily round as when the class has to clear away a multitude of materials after a creative activity period or when the children are changing before or after PE. At such times, considerable hubbub and confusion can arise as the children are occupied on different tasks at different places about the room at different rates. I have found it helpful at such times to start off a nursery rhyme and encourage the children to join in. The children suggest their favourites which are taken up by the rest of the class in a miniature 'top of the pops'. What could be a few moments of confusion, idle chatter or disruptiveness, punctuated by directions and instructions from the teacher, becomes an orderly and enjoyable occasion in which all the children, whether or not they have jobs to do, can participate. Such occasions provide opportunities for incidental teaching and repetition. New nursery rhymes should be taught directly to the class as a whole and opportunities should be taken for the class, in unison as well as individually, to repeat them. When each rhyme is mastered the teacher should ensure that the children understand the words in their context and that they can retell the title, the story and the moral (if any) in their own words.

Probably the earliest writing and reading that children will meet will be the content of the familiar nursery rhymes in caption form accompanying pictures in sequence.

Other rhymes which I have found particularly helpful, especially for eaching important directional and positional concepts, are the thirty or so action rhymes which are interspersed through the manual to Stott's *Flying Start Learning to Learn Kit*.

Teach Them to Speak

There are a number of oral language teaching kits on the market and because they include various amounts of hardware, all are expensive, some excessively so. Though I am no enemy to structure, I am aware that many commercial kits are so heavily programmed that many teachers find them confining and see little scope for initiative and spontaneity. Again as the materials are produced for a mass market of hypothetical five to eight year olds, teachers naturally question their relevance for the thirty or so particular children whom they happen to be teaching at any given moment. With these factors in mind I would like to recommend Shiach's admirable book *Teach Them to Speak* (Shiach 1972). The major part of the book consists of 200 daily lesson plans. Each plan suggests materials which may be used and gives extremely detailed suggestions for treatment of each lesson topic. Throughout the accent is on practical activities directed at the encouragement of effective oral response in well-structured sentences. The procedures and techniques are aimed at children between three and eight years old. The book is full of ideas, each of which is developed extensively and teachers are encouraged to select rather than follow each programme slavishly. The structure is there for those who wish to use it but it is not intended as a straitjacket. Full suggestions are given about materials and their sources and most teachers could acquire those they need without undue difficulty. Using Shiach, teachers can operate a first-class language development programme tailored to the precise needs of their particular children at remarkably low cost.

Oral language and reading

Though the importance of oral language is increasingly recognized, there is need to give it still greater prominence in school curricula. Teachers of very small children are still notoriously prone to get children to put on paper language which they are incapable of expressing in speech. Speaking and listening are still the major means of communication and we must be on our guard to stress the primacy of speech, especially at this time when children in every way more immature than those we have taught before begin to swell our nursery/infant schools. In concentrating on oracy in our nursery and reception classes we shall, of course, be giving them the best possible means of making a successful start in reading. Words must be shown to be conveyors of meaning and if they have been met first in speech, then recognition and meaning are possible when reading begins. Reading is much more than mere recognition and words in phrases and sentences are more meaningful than words in isolation. The more the child is familiar with the basic rhythms and patterns of our language, the more he can rely on those structures to recur consistently. Such familiarity enables him to anticipate in context the actual structures of the printed text and thus to read not only early, given favourable conditions, but fluently as well. Where the child's stock of language patterns is impoverished it may be possible to teach him laboriously to decode word by word but not with fluency and understanding. (Readers unfamiliar with the concept of anticipation skills as the basis of fluency should consult chapter 4 of *Reading Development and Extension* (Walker 1974) where the matter is given detailed consideration.) It is for these reasons that, throughout this chapter, I have repeatedly stressed not vocabulary as such, but words expressed with the rhythm, pattern and structure of clear, simple sentences. There is no point in making beginning reading any harder than it already is and if we are to teach reading at all, we should aim at fluency and understanding rather than barking ↑ print. If there is a moral in this chapter it is surely this – before we te' ↑ read, let us first teach them to speak.

References
SHIACH, G. (1972) *Teach Them to Speak* Lond   Educational
WALKER, C. (1974) *Reading Development a*   idon: Ward
     Lock Educational

Chapter 6

Emotional factors

Most teachers of small children will be aware that, despite carefully programmed and most sensitive attention to visual, auditory and oral language factors, some children just do not learn. They appear to have sufficient perceptual and linguistic equipment to cope satisfactorily with life in general, but do not apply it to learning in school. They are obviously maladjusted to school but whether it is to school itself, or what the school has to offer, or the tasks expected of them, or to all or only some of these things, is often extremely difficult to judge. Maladjustment is manifested in various ways, in varying degrees of severity and has a variety of causes, many of which are beyond the power of teachers to influence or control. The more teachers are aware of the different ways in which maladjustment is manifested, the more they are able to identify at least those children who are at risk as potential nonreaders. With sensitive handling by teachers, minor problems of adjustment can be overcome. It is possible to cushion the transition from home to school by certain organizational procedures and there is undoubted need to build more bridges between the two environments than exist at present. However, some children suffer from emotional handicaps of such severity that no infant schools, no matter how enlightened and concerned, can hope to induce learning without much greater resources than they are permitted to deploy at the present time.

What schools can do

Preschool parental education
In the first place, schools could make much more strenuous efforts to influence the attitudes of parents of preschool children than they do currently. The majority of children are enrolled many months, sometimes years, before the actual date of starting school. Local demographic surveys by school attendance and welfare personnel give detailed information about likely school starts. Such information could be pooled more effectively than it is now so that schools would know well ahead not only their catchment areas but exactly whom they will catch and when. It

should be possible to circularize the majority of parents of preschool children with a small booklet giving information about the school's aims and policies, as well as practical hints as to how parents themselves can help to promote school readiness. Such advice might encourage parents to ensure that children can dress or undress for PE and be able to cope with buttons, shoe-laces and the like; that they have experience of pencils, scissors, paint and crayons; that they are read to each bedtime and spend some part of each day talking about what they do with one or both parents. They can be encouraged to count the stairs on their way to bed and discuss the size (big, little, etc) of helpings at meal times. There are some things we should ask parents *not* to do; they should refrain from teaching the children the alphabetic names of the letters. If in doubt on any of these or similar matters, parents should be encouraged to call in at school to talk them over with school staff. Parents should certainly have at least one personal interview with the head some weeks before their child starts school. Here the head can ascertain at first hand if pupils have any physical or other defects which may impede learning, or whether special medical or dietary treatment has been prescribed. Often teachers have to find these things out for themselves and minor defects are frequently discovered when the child has been in school for some time and has already 'switched off' from learning.

Prestart visits
Parents should be encouraged to bring their preschool children to school occasionally to get them used to the new environment in which they will later have to spend a number of years. To many children the world of school is so different from what they have been accustomed to that a period of gentle conditioning is necessary. Schools must seem bewilderingly large, crowded, noisy and bustling to the child who lives in the ivory tower of a high rise block of flats and who has rarely experienced the luxury of playing or being with even the smallest group of other children. Often such acclimatization is achieved informally as the baby accompanies his mother each morning and afternoon to school, taking or meeting older brothers and sisters. Over a period of time the preschooler could expect to have met informally all the members of the school staff and to be familiar with the geography of the building and with some of the activities which take place within it. However, only children or eldest children would not normally acquire such experience and more formal acclimatization arrangements should be planned by the school as deliberate policy. These could include invitations to parties, plays, school assembly or to occasional painting or free play sessions. Invitations could be staggered so that not too many preschoolers have to be coped with at one time.

Though matters are improving, I am constantly reminded that collaboration between home and school is not universally effective by the number of schools I visit which still display notices to the effect that 'No parent is allowed beyond this point'. Some parents are undoubtedly very trying. They are fussy, overassertive, overprotecting. There is the well-known story of the headmistress who had a recurring dream, after which she invariably awoke with her face wreathed in smiles. She kept dreaming she was the head of an orphanage. However, when parents seem overfussy we cannot just close our eyes and pretend that they have gone away. The reason for their frequent visits will usually reflect a genuine concern for the progress and well-being of their children. They need to be reassured that the school is doing a good job. In all that we do we should be proving to them that they may have confidence in us. They pay us, equip us and entrust to us their children, without whom we would all be unemployed. In return we should go out and 'sell ourselves' to them.

Starting school

Some years ago I was the head of a very large infant and junior school into which, each year, I had to admit some 120 reception age children. I felt hamstrung in those days by the need to take each child in the term when he was five on the first day of the school term. One September, fifty-eight children had to start school on the same day. I was not permitted any sort of flexibility about staggering the arrangements. My heart bled at the tears and distress of so many little ones. The whole thing reminded me of those huge lorries crammed with pitiful cattle on their way to the abattoir.

Nowadays schools are allowed much greater flexibility in their admission arrangements. It makes sense to stagger the admissions over a week or two, taking a few children each day and settling them in happily to a good start. However, once we have got them in, things are far from perfect. I believe that for small children full-time attendance at school, right from the start, is too much of a strain. They are overtired by the many demands made on their effort and concentration during a long school day. If, in the first term, they had to attend either mornings only or afternoons only, the transition from home to school would not be so abrupt. Class sizes could be halved at one stroke. This would result in teachers being able to give more individual attention to children than is now possible and teaching would thereby become much more effective. We could also expect children's attention to be more highly geared to effective learning than it is now.

Starting school 'equally'

Those parents who are fortunate enough to have their children born in the autumn months can almost guarantee that their children will do well in school. Children born in the summer months rarely have such success. If all parents knew what an important educational factor the child's date of birth is, we could end up with a national 'close season' for procreation, which would result in all children being born between 1st September and 31st December. In present conditions, such children have a full three years in the infant school. Children born in the spring term have $2\frac{2}{3}$ years, while those born in summer have from $2\frac{1}{3}$ maximum to a bare 2 years, in some cases, of infant education. Thus an autumn-born child could have had half as much education again as the summer-born child by the time that *both* of them go on the same date to the same junior school.

This iniquitous inequality results from LEA policies which require infant schools to admit children, according to birthdates, in September, January or April. What seems to me particularly unjust is that it is only the infant school which is afflicted with such an administrative burden. I wonder how junior and secondary schools would cope if their first year entrants came at three different times in the year. It should be national policy to guarantee to all children a full three years of infant schooling. This can only be done by having all children start school at the beginning of the school year in which they will be five years old. This is particularly important from the point of view of learning to read. Autumn-born children have a full three years to get through the infant reading programme. Children with summer birthdays have only two years. With the latter, teachers are aware that they will soon be juniors and there is undue pressure on both children and teachers to achieve standards of literacy commensurate with junior school education. Teachers feel obliged to take short cuts. What should need three years has to be cut down to two. Consequently, prereading tends to be cursorily treated or omitted altogether and children are faced with reading tasks which are beyond them. They fail right at the beginning and 'switch off' from books and hence from almost all forms of learning in school.

A reception year
When one considers all that has to be done to get *all* children ready to make a good start in both reading and writing, it is obvious that some forms of organization will accomplish this better than others. I regard it as essential for every child to spend a full year in a reception class. Given three full years of infant education for each child, it should be much easier to consider the first year as the reception year than it is at present. Because schools are frequently forced to admit children at three different times of the year, some children are pushed up into a higher class for no better reason than to make room for new children coming in lower down. Thus

the small child is deprived of the security and stable relationship with his teacher which he needs more than anything else in his first year. After a term or so with one teacher he has to adjust, if he can, to a completely new person, in a different setting, with different attitudes, ideas and expectations from those to which, for a brief spell, he has just grown accustomed. The teacher also has to adjust to the new children and has to learn about them almost from scratch.

The first year in school is a decisive year, one in which the majority of children should develop a good learning style and, in particular, get off to a good start in reading and writing. For this purpose, the first year should be regarded as an observation year in which a gradual transition from home to school is effected and in which all those factors which particularly affect reading should be observed, recorded and positively handled. One cannot observe the beginnings of growth towards literacy and therefore influence these most favourably without the ability to observe the child in a variety of learning situations and within a time scale of less than one year. As has been indicated earlier, the teacher does not merely wait for indicators of readiness to manifest themselves in children; rather by the provision of suitably graded activities and experiences the teacher accelerates the process and begins the formal process of teaching reading at the optimum moment. This presupposes on the part of the teacher a certain specialist orientation towards the prereading rather than the beginning end of the early reading continuum. Such an orientation itself presupposes more specific teacher training of a nursery/infant rather than infant/junior type. Prereading also requires a set of practices, approaches, materials and equipment which are quite different from those suitable for the developing reader.

Many schools adopt vertical grouping as one way round their admission problems. It is admittedly easier to absorb into each class in the school a few new children each term rather than cram them into a reception class. Whether this is the best thing for the youngest children themselves is debatable. In theory they are helped in many ways by the other children. I can't help feeling that they could be helped much more effectively by specialist teachers in specialist rooms where all is specifically geared to the five year old. It would also be a rare teacher who is equally at home with five year olds as she is with seven year olds. When I myself taught vertically-grouped infant classes I was frequently conscious that my top infants would soon be juniors and that they needed a great deal of my attention if they were to leave me shortly, fitted to cope with junior school. I don't think I was a particularly bad teacher, but I certainly found it difficult to cope with every group at once. Realistically I had to regard my class as a series of layers each at a different level of competence in reading. The sooner I worked my top group up to independence, the sooner I could work my next batch up to the same level. My anxiety to get the older children on was not assuaged by the certain knowledge that if they left unable to read there was no one in junior school with the experience, training, or expertise to develop them further as readers. All this left my poor little five year olds very much out in the cold. There was also constant difficulty in hitting the right level with PE, movement, creative work and even in selecting a story which would interest my fives without boring my sevens. Everything had to be done either individually or in small groups. With a reception class there are frequent occasions when they can be taught as a class, in fact this is probably the only time in school where class teaching is profitable. When class teaching is possible it means that a lot of ground can be covered with maximum economy. As the children develop they diverge more each year, so that class teaching is ineffective as the spread of individual differences and abilities widens.

Many teachers have experienced, as I have, the difficulties of coping with vertically-grouped classes. Nowadays, with somewhat reduced class sizes, things may be a little easier. Even so, the multiplicity of teaching roles and goals makes it difficult for teachers to avoid feelings of guilt that they are neglecting some sections of their classes. With today's class sizes such feelings are always probable no matter how children are organized. However, vertical grouping is for many only an expedient which covers up the fact that in order to educate our five year olds effectively we need better provision than we now have. Children are only five once and their needs are different from those of other age groups. Not only do they need reception classes, the classes need to be kept small. No reception class should have more than twenty children. It should be staffed by one specialist trained teacher and one teacher's aide. The younger the child, the more demands he makes on the teacher's time, attention and ability. Older children who can read and write do not depend on their teachers for help at every second of every day as do school beginners. We encourage maladjustment when class sizes are too big and adjustment problems have the most far-reaching consequences at the very beginning of schooling. The more like home the school is, the more easily will the small beginner adjust to it and feel happy and secure within it. A class with upwards of twenty children must seem more like a factory than a home to the child just starting school. As for open-plan buildings, with their apparently built-in noise, bustle and distraction, they must appear to be the least likely places from which the five year old, barely loosed from his mother's apron strings, will derive the confidence with which to launch himself upon the world.

Observing and guiding learning behaviour

So far in this chapter I have considered how school organization can reduce feelings of tension and anxiety in children starting school. This is essential if children are to learn effectively and there are enough difficulties in learning to read without adding to them by maladministration or lack of sensitivity. However, no matter how we organize ourselves to help children, there will be some who suffer from handicaps of temperament which affect their ability to learn effectively. Probably very few children make the maximum use of their abilities but those with emotional handicaps are particularly prone to failure in reading. The question is, do they necessarily have to fail? From the point of view of reading, the major thesis of this book is that a greater consideration of what is involved in prereading encourages teachers to identify those children who are likely to be at risk. They are at risk because they do not try at all, or if they do try they either do not try hard enough or try in the wrong ways. Frequently we judge from the way in which a child reacts to learning that he does not have the ability. How certain can we be that this judgment is correct? It could well be that he has the ability, but is just not using it or is misusing it. All we can say with certainty is that he does not appear to be learning, that he is using faulty learning strategies, or is developing bad learning habits. Our job is to teach reading, not to fail at it, so in order to do the job it is first necessary to be able to recognize those children with poor learning styles and then to set about correcting them. We need to change the child's attitude from 'I can't' to 'I can', or from 'I won't' to 'I want to'.

Recognizing and counteracting the 'I can't' attitude

When a child gives us the impression that he cannot do the tasks we set him, he is simply expressing lack of confidence in himself. This is usually demonstrated outwardly either by timidity or withdrawal. In either case he appears to produce little in the way of energy applied to the learning task. The stimuli produce an underreaction.

The timid child

The timid child may not necessarily be the same as a withdrawn child. The timid child is best considered by looking at those aspects of behaviour encompassed in a continuum from unassertive to assertive. In the first place we have to consider the degree of timidity which a child exhibits. Many children, probably through lack of appropriate experience, are afraid to approach what is for them a new learning situation. They are easily helped by gentle encouragement, by breaking down the learning steps into simple stages and by being given ample practice at each stage so that they feel sufficiently confident to tackle the next small step. In time, the mildly timid child can be conditioned, by suitably programmed experiences, to get the feeling 'I can do it'.

There are children whose timidity is much more pronounced. They need much deeper teacher support than the mildly afraid and every response has to be coaxed out of them. Where the mildly timid can often work on their own at a suitable level, or can be helped by working and playing with peers, children whose fears lie deeper benefit from more individual teacher time and attention and will require a longer programme of prereading activity. It is for children such as these that I regard a year in a reception class as vital. They cannot be rushed into reading and need a long and stable relationship with a sympathetic adult who observes and helps them all the way. Such help cannot be provided if classes number more than twenty children.

The withdrawn child
Withdrawal is frequently on a different behaviour plane from timidity and is best viewed on a continuum from introvert to extrovert. The introvert is self-sufficient, copes well with school and is often the ideal student. We all tend to become introverts prior to examination time. Few teachers complain about those well-adjusted people who quietly get on with their work, make progress, listen attentively, and yet can make significant contributions to classwork when asked or when there is a need for it. It is only when withdrawal results in faulty learning that there is cause for worry. It is quite common for small children who are unaccustomed to playing with others to need time to acclimatize themselves towards the need to cooperate. They take refuge in their own company. When faced with new problems they show little initiative. Their play is solitary and repetitive. With a little encouragement they can in time be integrated with their fellows and learn from them new and more effective learning strategies. It is better at first to encourage them to play in pairs and when they have developed confidence here to gradually introduce them to working and playing in larger groups. It is obvious, too, that they must gradually gain experience of a wide variety of learning experiences and will require longer at prereading than normal, well-adjusted children.

Some children soon grow used to opting out. They adopt a fixed pattern of working and can only be induced to vary it with a lot of teacher support. The more withdrawn child's restricted learning strategies result in behaviour which can only be described as bizarre. Still, given time, a wide and lengthy prereading programme, and considerable attention from his teacher, his behaviour can be modified. He need not fail in reading.

The 'apparently' dull child

Many a confidence-lacking child behaves in learning situations as if he is really dull. However, the appearance of dullness is belied when in other aspects of daily life he copes quite well and indeed, on most occasions, he seems to behave very sensibly. Is his dullness a shield, a refuge into which he retreats like a tortoise into its shell when danger threatens? Is the danger really that he does not want to get involved? We do not help such children by accepting their opinion of themselves at face value and fatalistically assuming that they are dull and that therefore they are not going to read. If we accept this we will fail as well. We help them best by frequent praise and constant encouragement, by making the learning steps so small that they have success at every stage. This again presupposes a varied prereading programme, small classes and stable teacher–pupil relationships.

Some children, if allowed to 'play dumb' for too long, learn that it pays to establish a reputation as a slow learner. This guarantees them a comfortable existence. They are absolved from work or strenuous effort, are not expected to answer questions, listen or give attention. Occasionally, however, when off their guard, these shammers show flashes of brightness. We should fasten onto these rare manifestations to let them see that we have spotted their little game. They are better kept busy, with plenty to do, and we must make certain that what we ask is done. This will require a lot of our time, but it is often a battle of wills. We must insist that they come up to the standards we set. We must show them that our will for them to succeed is greater than their will to fail. Parental support for school policies is a very useful prop in such cases.

Severe underreaction

In the instances cited above I have attempted to indicate that a certain amount of timidity, withdrawal or apparent dullness need not result in reading failure. By preparing the way, by protecting children from too sudden an approach to formal reading, by reasonable provision, by good organization, and particularly by sensitive teacher help, much possible failure can be prevented. However, some children demonstrate a lack of confidence so severe that they cannot be helped in the normal school without a considerable augmentation of resources.

Some children are so excessively fearful that they behave as though turned to stone when confronted by any new learning situation. Extreme withdrawal can result in behaviour so 'way out' that the simplest problems cannot be tackled by means even remotely realistic. Again, some children are so determined, and probably quite unconsciously so, not to get involved that they appear quite helpless in any situation which requires them to make the slightest effort. They pursue their solitary, eccentric routines in a pattern so fixed and repetitive that no amount of persuasion will induce them to vary their strategies in order to cope with different situations. In all such cases of severe underreaction, infant schools in our country are faced with impossible tasks. Children thus handicapped require so inordinate an amount of teacher time and attention that the brighter and more normal children can be quite neglected if appropriate help is to be given to those in real distress. With such children, teachers can easily get out of their depth. Teachers are not psychologists. Their strengths are in the cognitive field and, though through training and experience they may acquire acute psychological insights, there are limits to the amount of help they can give, unaided, when faced with grave abnormality.

In theory, there is machinery, the schools psychological service, for providing help for the hard-pressed teacher. Such help, when it is given, is of two main kinds. Firstly, in the case of the underreacting child whose problems are pronounced though not quite severe, the psychologist tests and diagnoses, works on the spot and in conjunction with the school staff, and suggests appropriate action within the ordinary school. Secondly, in severe cases the children may be removed from the ordinary school to a special school. I might add that, in the case of infant school children, help of either kind is rarely given. This may be due to LEA policies which restrict the expansion and resources of the school psychological service so that it cannot cope with the incessant demands made upon it. This is usually the case. Also, heads of infant schools are notoriously reluctant to ask for whatever outside help is available. Such reluctance is partly understandable if heads are well aware that the psychologists are hard-pressed. It is a common experience to have to wait months, and often years, for the psychologist to take up cases referred to him, by which time the children in question, referred as infants, are well up in the junior school. There is little point in asking for help which you are not going to get when it matters. On the other hand, many heads accept fatalistically that the emotionally disturbed, like the poor, are always with us. They are vaguely optimistic that time will cure all ills. Such optimism is unfounded. The child goes deeper into trouble the longer his problems remain untreated. Nor do class teachers scream for help as loudly and as frequently as they should. The underreacting child is usually quiet, well-behaved, odd maybe, but not disruptive. As he causes few disciplinary problems he tends to produce an underreaction from his teachers, i.e. general sympathy and mild concern. This should be contrasted with the very energetic responses which teachers make to children who are hostile, aggressive and disruptive. Here the attitude can be expressed as 'I must get them learning or I shall never have a minute's peace and none of the other children will learn anything either'.

Whatever the reasons, in our British infant schools we allow children to go on failing far too long before any outside agencies are brought in to help. While this attitude persists, we are forcing our teachers, especially the young and inexperienced, to take decisions which they are not competent to make and forcing them into situations in which they, too, are almost certainly bound to fail.

Identifying and dealing with the 'I won't' attitude

The children who exhibit the 'I can't' attitude tend to be passive. Those who implicitly say 'I won't' usually give the impression that they could, if only they wanted to. They are usually quite active in resisting learning and expend considerable amounts of energy in demonstrating their reluctance. Such overabundance of energy stems from handicaps of temperament which discourage learning by an overreaction to the task or avoidance of it. Such energetic behaviour provokes equally energetic responses from teachers for these children unconsciously make no bones about wanting attention and their behaviour guarantees that they get it.

The 'butterfly' child

Some children seem unable to settle down to any worthwhile task for longer than a few seconds. They have great difficulty in concentrating and are easily distracted. They will attend to almost anything except the task in hand. Even when pinned down to some definite learning activity by individual teacher attention, they show a remarkable capacity for attending to some irrelevant aspect of the material. When asked to look closely at a symbol in a matching card they will point to a tear or a mark on the card. Just when they seem to have got the point and be 'with us' they suddenly look up and find some object in the classroom on which to focus attention.

They become much more of a nuisance when they do not keep their distractions to themselves but, by creating unnecessary diversions, disrupt the learning of those around them. Now it is obvious that many children, before starting school, have no experience of attending to anything closely or for fairly long periods. Again, on first coming to school, many children are going to be confronted by objects and activities of such bewildering variety, profusion and novelty that they will need some time to take everything in and get used to the new environment. Given all this, there are some who demonstrate their 'butterfly' tendencies far beyond any reasonable settling-in period and we cannot allow them to get away with it for our own sake, for theirs and for the sake of those around them. Such children can only be helped individually and with some firmness. We have to insist that they complete the work we set. At first the tasks will be simple and will not take long. We will need to sit with them, give them some encouragement, but stay there until the job is done. The learning gradient will become steeper, the tasks more complex, as they develop the power to concentrate harder and longer. To give the sort of teacher attention which these children need requires far smaller classes than we have at present.

There are, however, children whose distractibility is so severe that they continually disrupt the work of the entire class. When all reasonable attempts at coping with such children have been made, schools should not delay in seeking the additional help which the school psychological service can provide.

The 'fidget'

Some hyperactive children do not seem able to sit still for longer than a few seconds. To them an ordinary, innocent chair becomes a bed of nails. They are almost febrile in the way in which first one, than another part of their bodies is in constant movement. Such children are difficult to cope with when they can confine themselves to their chairs, albeit in a state of perpetual motion. Such overactivity impedes their own capacity to learn as well as being a constant source of distraction to others. They are worse when they cannot sit at all but take to wandering about the room. We must accept that active, healthy children on starting school are going to find much classroom routine irksome and confining. Most infant schools go along with this natural tendency by encouraging methods which channel the child's desire for activity into learning pursuits. Great care is given to a balanced programme in which intense physical activity which allows the children to let off steam alternates with quieter pursuits in which the children can listen and attend. In time the majority of children can be so conditioned. Some take longer than others and for these the planning of special materials and activities, as well as the individual help needed to work at them, takes up a great deal of the teacher's time and professional skill if success is to be achieved.

There are, however, those excessively hyperactive children who do not respond to the treatment that ordinary teachers are able to provide. They cannot sit at all but flit from activity to activity and from place to place throughout each school day, leaving a constant trail of distraction in their wake. Teachers should not attempt the impossible for long but should refer such children in the first place to the school medical service. For some, the prescription of mild sedation with the teacher cooperating in its administration is often sufficient to slow them down, so that learning can begin. Others may require treatment of a much more sophisticated kind under clinical conditions which necessitate withdrawal from the normal school.

In all the cases cited so far the teacher's professional judgment is under great strain. She has the constant responsibility for making decisions which vitally affect all her children. She has to observe and record, structure programmes and materials, help and encourage until she has to take the ultimate decision – should she continue under her own steam with limited time and resources or should she scream for outside help from agencies which she knows to be as hard-pressed as herself? In severe cases she is the active link between constant parental consultation and many different agencies such as the school medical or psychological service or the family doctor. She needs far more time, i.e. much smaller classes, if children in difficulty are to get the help they need. If such children do not get helped either by or through the teacher, all the other children are liable to suffer educationally through the disruption generated by the emotionally disturbed. The teacher who has to give inordinate attention to one child has all the less time to devote to all the other children.

The aggressive child

Many children are aware of the difference between play and work, no matter how cunningly the latter is disguised. They react towards work in a hostile way, become moody when set a task and often refuse to get started. In cases of mild hostility, it is often sufficient to make the task appealing, give praise and responsibility or alternatively be firm and insist that the work is done in exchange for some immediate reward such as extra play or choice of subsequent activity. It would be an unusual small child who did not have the occasional tantrum and such behaviour poses no major problem for teachers.

When petulance is persistent, the teacher's task is more difficult. She has to spend a lot of time observing strengths and weaknesses. She has to get to know the child from every angle for it may well be that in some respects the work she is setting really is too hard. If this is so, she will have to break the work down into smaller steps in order to give the child confidence and to make the chance of success at each stage more certain. Sometimes a child will get over his initial refusal to start, but as soon as the going gets rough, hostility sets in. He may react violently against the materials or refuse to cooperate with his partner in a game. It may be that what he really needs is a greater share of our patience and attention and we do him no good by withholding them. In time, the majority of such children learn to relax their antagonism and realize it pays to try and to experience the joy of a job well done.

Some, however, always react to pressure in a violently aggressive manner. Every task brings about an angry confrontation. They not only refuse to work but scatter the material about, damage it, or vent their spleen on the children about them. Frequently they demonstrate their hostility with their feet and will run out of the room altogether. Such persistent outbursts place the other children under great strain. In my experience, infant school personnel tolerate such behaviour in a well-meaning way for too long. All the reactions of the violently aggressive child are danger signals which the poor child is flashing to us, indicating to us that he is badly in need of help. If we cannot help him we should lose no time in calling in those who can.

The cases of emotional difficulty which I have cited are by no means a comprehensive list. They are merely a sample of some quite common types of behaviour with which the ordinary teacher has to deal every day in the typical infant class. Nor have I attempted to indicate the reasons why certain children behave as abnormally as they do. I have merely pointed out the sorts of problems that have to be met. Frequently the difficulties which I have indicated are compounded by multiple personality defects. For example, the violently aggressive child might be fidgety and butterfly-minded as well.

The fact that many children do have handicaps of temperament certainly complicates the business of getting *all* the children ready for reading. These particular children are at very grave risk for there is no doubt in my mind that if the children cannot, or will not make the effort, i.e. have an emotional blockage towards learning, all other contributory factors such as high intelligence, well developed powers of visual and auditory perception, and good oral language facility will not help them to make a start on reading. Frequently the emotionally defective child also suffers from deprivation in those other areas mentioned as essential for reading readiness. Of one thing we can be sure: children with emotional difficulties will not come to reading easily and will need much more prereading activity than more normal children.

Implications for the infant school

The matters raised in this chapter have many implications for the infant school:

1   Getting a group of children ready to read is a difficult business because of the many aspects of development which have to be taken into account. In the past we have tended to put children on books too soon. Instead of merely awaiting readiness, however, we should attempt to accelerate the process by varied programmes of prereading activity

rather than by slogging away to no avail at the formal beginnings of reading centred on books.

2 In almost every infant class there are some children who, because of handicaps of temperament, require an inordinate amount of teacher time and attention. In present conditions the teacher cannot give these children the constant support which they need and, at the same time, cope with the other children who could be expected to make normal progress. Thirty should be the maximum number with which infant teachers should have to cope. Reception classes, however, pose special problems. The children are immature, have a short concentration span and for so many of their needs require direct teacher attention throughout the school day. Therefore, twenty children should be the maximum number in the reception class.

3 The reception class should be upgraded and regarded not merely as a place where the children are settled in, but as a setting specifically designed for five year olds, in which the children can be observed and their weaknesses diagnosed and treated in order to eliminate possible failure in reading. To achieve this the children should be guaranteed the most secure and stable relationships possible. They should have a full year with the one teacher.

4 The reception class teacher should also be upgraded. She should be freed from the many nonteaching chores which currently take up a great deal of her teaching day. These could be done by a full-time teaching aide, releasing the teacher to exploit her professional skills exclusively. She should be fully occupied in ensuring that each child learns to the limits of his potential.

5 Infant schools need more money for materials and equipment. It is quite unfair to the small child to assume that just because he is small less money may be spent on educating him than is spent on educating older children. There are good commercially-produced materials about but infant teachers are conditioned to improvising and making their own, rather than buying them. They are used to not having the money to buy what they need. Consequently, the vast majority of infant teachers suffer considerable personal expense and give up leisure time to make the tools with which to do their job. This does not happen to any great extent in junior or secondary teaching. Why should it be expected of infant teachers?

Implications for teacher training

Teacher training is becoming more specialized. Some years ago one trained for infant, or junior, or secondary teaching. More recently the need for some overlap between these categories has been reflected in courses labelled infant/junior, junior/middle, and junior/secondary. The emergence of the middle school has recently resulted in a number of courses labelled 'teaching in middle schools'. The most recent growth in the training institutions has been in the provision of nursery/infant courses. Many colleges are at this very moment endeavouring to recruit the staff to man and organize such courses. This is a new and rapidly growing area and many colleges are in the first stages of planning syllabuses for the first intakes of students. Hopefully prereading will be a prominent feature in their training. There is a danger that if the work is slanted more to the nursery than to the infant end of the spectrum, there is likely to be an overemphasis on the unstructured play and socialization which has characterized nursery work in the past. If the emphasis is placed more on the infant than on the nursery aspect, the danger is that there will be an overemphasis on formal reading, the use of reading schemes and the like. The nursery/infant teacher has the chance to bridge the gap between these extremes and her training should equip her to teach the skills and provide the experiences which enable her pupils to make a good start in reading.

Implications for LEA supporting services

There is a need to expand considerably LEA services such as medical and psychological support. Failure to do this will result in teachers having to overcome difficulties for which they have neither adequate training nor resources. There is also a need to change the whole direction and rationale of the supporting services. At the present time when outside help is given, it is almost always applied too late, i.e. when the children have already failed. The expensive superstructure of the various remedial services is then called upon. Almost all workers in the remedial service complain that their case loads are too heavy and that the help they can provide is therefore superficial, infrequent and unsuccessful.

We should aim, in the first place, at decimating the remedial service so that there is adequate help available but only for those children whose handicaps are so severe that they cannot be taught successfully in the ordinary schools. The money saved by a really drastic pruning of the remedial service could then be applied to its reorganization as a preventive service and to improving staffing ratios and teaching resources in infant schools, particularly in the reception year. Given the expansion in nursery schooling which successive governments have recently promised, a much expanded psychological service, whose *raison d'être* is essentially preventive, could then concentrate its efforts on the age group in which preventive work can be most effective, i.e. when the children are between four and six years old. We need many more educational psychologists and even more psychological social workers. The psychologists need to be freed from their many administrative burdens in order to be able to concentrate on:

1 Diagnosing and treating educational difficulties in school.
2 Giving on the spot advice and help to teachers in particular cases where
  pupils' abnormalities are not so severe that they cannot be handled in the normal school.
3 Evaluating new methods, approaches and materials for the benefit of teachers in their area.
4 Providing in-service training locally in identifying, testing, diagnosing and treating children likely to fail in school.

To discharge these important roles the psychologist needs to oversee a group of schools. The links between the schools and the psychologist would be a team of PSWs. I would like to see the PSWs visiting our schools every day. I would like to see them not as the last resort in a dire emergency, but as out looking for business, visiting homes and counselling their own small case load of children with problems. Finally, the psychologist should head a team of preventive teachers specially trained in prereading who could teach the most severe cases individually and get them ready to read.

Will the day ever come when, once a month, in every infant school there will be a meeting, chaired by the head, of the psychologist, the PSWs, the preventive teachers and the school teaching staff, reviewing progress and planning the next month's programme for those children in need of special help? When that day comes, we can be certain that we really are determined to eradicate failure in reading.

Chapter 7

Teaching the letters

Many teachers would question the need, in a book on prereading, for a chapter on teaching the letters. Indeed, many question the value of teaching the letters at all, either because they consider them far too difficult for small children, or because they believe the children, by some miraculous and unspecified means, will learn them all by themselves without any definite teaching. I am convinced that the letters need to be taught and taught very thoroughly before the children meet them in words, i.e. before they read.

Children who do know their letters have a great advantage in early reading and writing over those who are taught exclusively by whole word and sentence methods. Merely to know the first letter of a word eliminates a number of possibilities and, by tuning the child in accurately on the word the author intended him to recognize, much wild guessing is discouraged. To know the end sound as well is a further aid to recognition denied to those accustomed only to sight methods. With the many small words which characterize early reading there only remains the need to sort out the sound in the middle and independent reading can be said to have begun. To deliberately deny small children the means of acquiring such early independence in attacking a great number of words seems an odd way to teach reading. It may seem old-fashioned to some to want to bring order and system into learning to read. We do this with number. Why should the teaching of reading be so unsystematic? By teaching a child his letters we can introduce him gradually to a great number of the sound patterns of our language. In time he can come to detect consistent relationships between letter groupings and certain sound patterns. He can begin to establish rules which he can successfully apply to the decoding of words which he has not met before. In helping a child to make generalizations we help him to bring order into what would otherwise be a discrete mass of unorganized percepts, and thus make his learning more effective. The teacher who does not teach children their letters has only one means at her disposal – repetition. Repetitive methods imply that children can only be treated as parrots and I regard such an attitude as insulting to small children, the majority of whom are far from birdbrained. They can bring intelligence as well as memory to learning and the more they can be encouraged to use the former, the more effective their learning style will be.

Many teachers equate teaching the letters with the dull drills which characterized phonic work many years ago. Today there are many interesting and active ways of teaching the letters and then blending them into syllables and words. Many of today's teachers assume that by concentrating on the parts (the separate words) the child will not give due attention to the whole (the content). They say that the child cannot attend to the overall meaning of the reading matter if he focusses on the separate pieces. However, must the child's thinking be concentrated on the content only? Is he not thinking, when he reasons out the form of new words and builds them up in sound order? The child who knows his letters can be trained to think at every step and his ability to attack new words with confidence gives him the keys to unlock the overall meaning of the passage. How frequently do children, who lack training in phonic analysis, come to an abrupt halt when faced with new vocabulary! The child who knows his letters before he meets them in words usually has little difficulty in writing freely and has few problems later with spelling.

I know a number of teachers who regard learning the letters as a task far beyond the power of most five year olds. I personally have not found it so. I have found it possible to teach forty-five children all their letters, both capital and lower case, and have them all started on a reading scheme during their first term in school. The average age of these children was four and three-quarter years. The success of ita and *Words in Colour* with preschool children is well-documented in research. With the 'talking typewriter' even two year olds have made considerable progress in reading. I am convinced that teachers find teaching the letters too difficult only because they do not have their hearts in the task, or have not had the relevant training or experience. Alternatively, they prefer to do other things instead, such as having the children parroting from books by sight methods only. In my experience, those teachers who succeed in teaching the letters (or the characters in the case of ita) invariably proceed on the basis of a letter a day with a good recap each Friday. What are we paid for if we admit that we cannot teach all the children just one fact each day?

When do we teach capital letters?
Even among teachers who are unanimous that the children must learn their letters, there is likely to be considerable disagreement as soon as capital letters are mentioned. In my work in in-service training with very experienced teachers, I am used to asking the question, 'If you don't teach

capital letters at the very beginning, when do you teach them?'. I am also used to hearing some very vague replies. Obviously we cannot defer them till the child has mastered the rules of capitalization. These same rules are certainly too difficult to teach at the very beginning of schooling. Probably the first words that a child will want to write are his name. Are we then to teach Billy Smith to identify himself as billy smith? Again, if we were using a certain well-known reading scheme, would we think of introducing its main characters as dick, dora, nip, fluff, jack and may? Probably the first connected writing which children meet formally will be sentences about some interesting happening in school. Will the teacher then write on the board for the children to 'read', 'today we got a guinea-pig. we called him billy'? There is only one way to avoid all such dilemmas – teach both the capital and lower case form of each letter at the same time. For 'capital' substitute 'big' and for 'lower case' say 'little'.

Matching the letters
Before actually learning the letter sounds the child must be familiarized with their visual forms. He must be able to recognize them by their visual characteristics and in order to do this will probably need some experience of matching and sorting the actual letter shapes. This, of course, would normally follow a progression of matching at more concrete levels as suggested in chapter 3. At the first stage of letter matching he will have a greater chance of success if his experience is limited to capital letter forms exclusively. These are much more distinctive than lower case letters and therefore form the obvious material for the first exercises in letter shape discrimination. Self-correcting posting activities are a traditional device which the children enjoy. They play at this in pairs, one child posting the letters, the other checking by a pictorial correcting symbol at the back. Any card posted in the wrong box is returned. The children play at this activity until they can match accurately every time. The teacher is thus freed from overseeing much work at the practice stage and need only be directly involved when each child feels completely competent with a given group of letters and asks the teacher to test him.

   Sixteen of the capital letters have a different form from their lower case counterparts. I usually introduce these right at the beginning by providing four letter boxes and sixteen cards, one for each letter:

Stage 1

A B D E   F G H I   J K L M   N Q R T

Many four year olds and nearly all five year olds can match simple letter shapes providing they attend to what they are doing and use their eyes. Apparatus such as the post box ensures that they do look closely. For extra motivation the child may take a counter each time he is right first time. This particular game can be played in pairs, the children taking turns with their partners at posting, then checking. Alternatively, a group of up to five children can be kept busy, one as postman, the other four each in charge of one of the boxes. They take turns at being the postman.

Stage 2
At stage 2, the children can be introduced to the lower case counterparts of the letters used in the first stage above. Four boxes, as shown, and sixteen cards for posting are required:

   a b f g   d h i k   j l n q   m r e t

Note that b, d and q have been allocated to different boxes to avoid early orientation confusions.

Stage 3
At stage 3 the ten letters whose capital and lower case forms are the same are introduced. Three letter boxes and ten cards are required:

   c o p   u v s   w x y z

The children can play at this activity either in pairs or in groups of four (one postman, three checkers).

Stage 4
At stage 4 the children are to match in pairs the letters which have different capital/lower case counterparts. Four boxes and sixteen cards are needed:

  Aa Bb Dd Ee   Ff Gg Hh Ii   Jj Kk Ll Mm   Nn Qq Rr Tt

Teaching the letter sounds
In the four activities described above, no attempt has been made to give a sound value to any of the letters presented. The various letter shapes have been used as the content in the final stage of a programme in visual discrimination only. When the children can match the letters accurately every time they are then ready to learn their correct sounds. Before suggesting how this stage may be tackled, I feel it necessary to give a number of warnings. I do so because many teachers responsible for teaching reception class children have not had specific training for the task. Many arrive in infant schools via secondary and junior teaching. Many of those specifically trained for work with infants may have had college

courses in which little emphasis was placed on phonic work. Whatever the reasons, I find that teaching the letters, when it is done at all, is often done very badly. The children are taught the wrong sounds. This is done in one of two ways. Firstly, a number of teachers teach the alphabetic names of the letters. Thus a child learns to spell 'cat' by making the sounds 'see ay tee'. More frequently an approximation to phonic sounds is attempted, but unfortunately the children are taught to voice the consonants. Here a sound equivalent to the e schwa in 'the' is added to the pure consonantal sound so that 'cat' is analysed as 'ker-a-ter'. In either case, if the letters are wrongly taught the child will not be able to blend them into words with the natural fleeting sounds as heard in speech. In the first place, therefore, it is essential not to teach the letters as isolated sounds, but as the beginning sounds of words within the children's experience. A further complication is the necessity to link one sound with two visual representations (capital and lower case) of sixteen of the letters of our alphabet.

There is no existing commercial apparatus in common use which attempts to overcome all these difficulties. The giant touch cards in Stott's *Programmed Reading Kit* (1971) only teach the lower case letters. Also it is difficult for teachers to handle more than two at a time. The folder-type cards recommended in the *Ladybird Key Words Manual*, and which, incidentally, the children are encouraged to make for themselves, are more easy to handle because they stand up by themselves. However, they are not designed for whole class teaching, nor do they teach the capital letters.

I have overcome all these problems successfully for more years than I care to remember by apparatus such as the *giant letter sounding cards* which will be incorporated in the Ward Lock Educational *Prereading Workshop*. Many hundreds of teachers trained by me at initial or in-service courses can also testify that they work. Below is a sample of a card designed to teach the short open vowel 'a' as it occurs as the beginning sound in 'ambulance'.

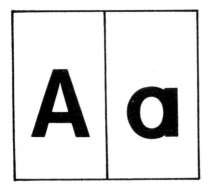

The card is folded down the dotted line so that it stands on the front of the teacher's desk. The class are seated in a semicircle, facing the picture. First, by discussion and observation, they learn the picture. They have to learn that it is an ambulance, not a van. Other pictures are introduced, one at a time, one for each of the other four short vowels. Each picture is 'learned'. At the end of this stage the children would see five cards showing respectively ambulance, egg, Indian, orange and umbrella, thus:

 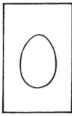   

When all the children know the names of the pictures they are withdrawn. The first two reappear but are reversed so that the children see only the letters, thus:

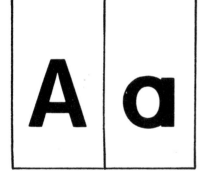 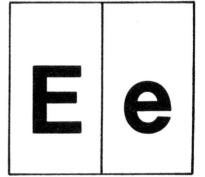

They are then invited to take turns at guessing which card has the ambulance, which the egg. They point to the card of their choice and check by reversing it to reveal the picture on the other side. When the majority are reasonably confident at this, the other cards are added one at a time, until the brighter children are right every time. These children then practise in pairs with smaller versions of the cards while the teacher works on with the slower ones.

By the end of this stage the children will still not have been given a sound value for the letters. They will only have learned to identify each picture visually by associating it with its beginning letter shape(s). When they can do this competently it is time to teach the sounds associated with the group of letters with which they are now familiar. Bring out the first two cards and present them to the children thus:

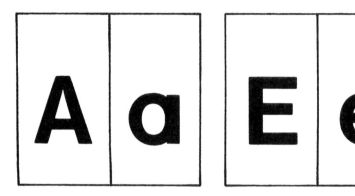

Say to one of the brighter children, 'I am going to say a word. The word is on the back of one of the cards. Point to the card where the word is. Are you ready?'. Then say, 'A' (the first sound in 'ambulance'). Reverse the card to which the child points to show the picture. If he is right, say, 'Good! I was going to say "ambulance"'. (Stress the 'a'.)

Repeat the procedure with the second card. Shuffle the cards round and give every child a chance. Be careful not to look at the card in question or the children may just follow your eyes instead of thinking. When the majority can link 'a' with 'ambulance' and 'e' with 'egg' every time, introduce the remaining cards in the group, one at a time, and repeat the procedures. The brighter children can then go off to practise in pairs with the smaller versions of the cards, taking a counter each time they are right, while the teacher continues working with the slower ones. This should continue until all the children know Aa for ambulance, Ee for egg, Ii for Indian, Oo for orange and Uu for umbrella.

The consonants can then be tackled in four groups of five sounds each (excluding the letter x, which is never a beginning letter in English). Each group could be separately colour-coded for ease of recording. For example, the short vowel cards referred to could all be white. The consonant groups could be organized as follows:

Bb	ball		Dd	dog	
Cc	coat		Jj	jug	
Ff	fish	} Yellow	Kk	key	} Red
Gg	goat		Ll	lion	
Hh	horse		Mm	milk	

94

Nn	nurse		Qq	queen	
Pp	policeman		Vv	van	
Rr	reindeer	Blue	Ww	watch	Green
Ss	sun		Yy	yacht	
Tt	table		Zz	zebra	

In order to avoid ambiguity, care should be taken to teach the pictures first, before associating them with letter shapes and finally teaching the sound values. Each group of five letters should be considered a week's work so that a letter a day is the aim. It is better to teach in short, sharp bursts of up to ten minutes. There should be three such bursts each day, punctuated by spells of quite different activity. Though the treatment should be regular, variety is essential to secure maximum motivation and concentration. The three separate teaching sessions a day could be organized thus:

1 Linking the pictures *visually* with the beginning letter shapes.
2 Giving the letters their correct sound values.
3 Writing the letters.

Much more care should be given to this aspect of literacy than is currently the case. If the teaching of beginning reading has become notoriously unsystematic, the teaching of handwriting is even more so. So many of today's teachers tend to let the children 'discover' everything for themselves and 'progress' (if that is the right word) through every aspect of learning at their own pace. How frequently do children make the wrong discoveries, and particularly in the case of handwriting, develop at the very start bad habits which make much of their later schooling ineffectual? Reading and writing do not come naturally. They are learned skills and therefore have to be taught. Ideally they should go hand-in-hand. In practice, writing almost invariably lags behind reading ability. Many children are left to pick up writing all by themselves, if they can. Without positive help they reinforce poor habits which make writing a slow, laborious, painful chore. No wonder so many children put pen to paper with such reluctance. Writing is an activity which takes up a great proportion of each school day. We ill prepare children for the long eleven years of compulsory schooling if we do not help them at the outset to establish the habits which help them to write with ease, speed and confidence.

I lay much of the blame for the difficulties which many children experience in handwriting on the workbook activities associated with look and say methods. The children copy whole words and get no help in forming the separate parts (the letters) of which the words are composed. Many children halfway through a reading scheme do not even know what letters are. The biggest impediment to progress in handwriting is the current emphasis on tracing whole words and sentences. The finished traced product gives no indication of the movements undertaken on the way. Many a piece of tracing which earns a sweet or a gold star has been written from right to left. Many a word 'was' has been started with the 'a', with the other letters added willy-nilly. How often will a child produce an apparently creditable 'a' but by a series of movements which go right against the grain. He starts with the vertical stroke, and frequently goes up and down the stroke several times. He takes his pencil off at the bottom of the stroke and goes from the vertical line to the curved line, starting at the bottom right-hand side. He may do this many times a day while his teacher remains aloof, thus cementing habits which are regressive and impede the natural flow of script. The child who learns to write entirely by tracing and copying whole words is faced with the task of reproducing many hundreds of different complex shapes. By a more structured, positive approach we could show him that such a task can be whittled down to learning just forty-two basic shapes, which comprise all the capital and lower case letters of our alphabet. Anyone who cannot teach these thoroughly in a few short weeks should not be licensed to teach small children.

There are various ways by which this task may be organized. Some teachers adopt the following sequence:

1   letters composed of straight lines
2   letters formed by curves
3   letters combining straight lines and curves

Another sequence goes as follows:

1   capital letters
2   'very small' letters
3   'small' ascenders
4   'small' descenders

Such organized approaches are not necessarily dull. Good teachers enliven the work by applying the basic skills to patterns which, though repetitive, become progressively more complex and which involve a variety of media, including chalk, crayons, paint and pencils.

I personally favour the 'letter a day' approach whereby, as mentioned earlier in this chapter, writing is the third and final stage in learning the letter of the day. I find that setting a daily target marvellously concentrates the teacher's mind and purposes. It is a considerable aid to recording progress. The recording itself indicates that some children need extra help and reminds the teacher to set some time aside for providing it for those in need, lest they fall behind. It also helps to keep the whole class together at this early stage. Learning a letter a day gives the children a sense of achievement. This is what they came to school for – to learn to read and write. They are reassured (and so are their parents) that this is what they are doing.

However we teach children to write we will only do this successfully if we bear in mind the stage of maturity which the average five year old has achieved. We must be aware of the problems he is likely to face and the equipment he can bring to bear to deal with them. Writing calls for very finely coordinated movements of the fingers and wrists. The typical five year old has little competence or experience of such skills. At first he writes with his whole arm and shoulder, a massive body movement. He will soon become tired by physical exertions involving such massive movement, so to begin with the earliest attempts should be kept short, while the shapes he is to reproduce should be kept big. To help him he needs very big materials for such large-scale efforts. In addition to the physical difficulties involved, we also have to consider how we can teach the habits which will help the child to form the letters correctly. I have never had much difficulty using the following procedure.

1 *Tracing in the air*
As an example let us take the shape 'ɑ'. The letter is drawn very big on the blackboard. I trace it with my hand a few times while the children watch. I then invite them to stretch out their writing hands and trace the letter in the air with me. I verbalize the movements and get the children to verbalize them with me: 'Start here, round, up, straight down, stop. Good! Again. Round . . .' etc.

2 *Using chalkboards*
When satisfied that the children are making the correct movements in sequence in the air, I then invite them to reproduce the shape on individual chalkboards with lumps of thick chalk. They can erase their efforts as often as is necessary. The aim should be to draw in swift bold strokes. I get around the class helping where necessary and making a note of those experiencing severe difficulty. These children will get extra practice later in the day and the worst cases will receive kinesthetic treatment by tracing my big sandpaper letter shapes with index fingers.

3 Incidental reinforcement

During the six weeks or so when the entire class is involved in learning to write their letters, painting time is devoted to copying patterns based on letter shapes. These range from simple repetitive line patterns to more complex all-over patterns. The graded use of large-squared paper enables the teacher to condense progressively the size of the very big shapes which the children make at first.

4 Weekly revision

Friday is 'writing workshop' day when all the letters learned during the week are practised and consolidated.

5 Names and addresses

The climax to the writing sessions comes when the majority of children have practised all the letter shapes and they are presented with a card on which is written their name and address. This is necessary to give some point to all this activity, as well as to give the children a sense of self-identity. Many children are not aware that they have a surname or of where they live. Few can resist the invitation to go on copying from the card until their writing is as good as mine.

Further reinforcement and extension

The value of devices such as the giant letter sounding cards in directly teaching letter recognition and sounds has already been mentioned. However, such large material is extremely versatile and can be used to provide a good deal of incidental reinforcement. As each group of five cards is mastered they can be permanently exhibited as part of a growing picture-alphabet frieze. The children can refer to this as models for extra handwriting practice, while those who have great difficulty getting pen to paper can use the symbols for kinesthetic support. The cards also supply handy reference and starting points for games of 'I Spy'. The material becomes even more versatile when several sets, duplicated on a smaller scale, are available for pupils working either in pairs or in small groups under a competent child leader.

If no other materials were available, there is a danger that some children might come to associate each letter only with the picture on its card, e.g. 'a' might be associated only with 'ambulance' and not with other words which start with the same sound. 'I Spy' is an invaluable means of extending the letter sound concepts. However, many children need visual as well as auditory support and need to be more personally and actively involved in extending their letter sound concepts, so it is useful to provide a second complete set of small letter sounding cards in which a different set of pictures is associated with the same letter groupings. The same colour coding for the second set of cards as that used in set 1 could be retained. The teacher could record the progress of each child by noting the colour of the cards with which he is working. By progressing through two such sets of cards as those below, the child is led to deduce that 'a' is not only the beginning sound of 'ambulance', but of 'axe' also. Frequent games of 'I Spy' would widen this concept further.

Who teaches what?
No doubt many adherents of the out and out child-centred school of thought will feel their hackles rising as they plough their way through this chapter. However, we can no longer perpetuate the fallacy that children will grow into reading and writing in their own good time if we merely surround them with books. One million adult illiterates in our country today disprove this theory. We must constantly remind ourselves that the job of the teacher is to teach. We do not teach children fullstop. We have to teach them something. Granted, there are many things which we could trust them to pick up for themselves. Literacy, however, is too precious a gift to leave to chance and requires a progressive ordering of skills and experiences which children cannot work out for themselves. Many need help all the way and we do not help them by standing aside and waiting until they are ready. Some never are.

There are some things which we, as a profession, could do better. We plunge our youngest and most inexperienced probationers into work with small children with the most inadequate preparation in prereading. We could well dispense with much of the academic study of education. Instead we should let this grow out of thoroughly professional training in the skills of teaching and organizing prereading with the needs of children in school firmly in mind.

The new nursery schools and classes may have a great deal to offer in the cause of early literacy if they rise to the challenge. Unfortunately, the history of the nursery movement in our country has been dominated by social and medical rather than educational considerations. Now that the teachers have taken over the nursery system, can more strictly educational aims become the driving force? Much of the early visual, auditory, manipulative and oral work discussed in this book is well within the capacity of preschool children. Indeed, many come from homes which provide such experience so well that the nursery schools of the past have not been able to compete with them. The new nursery schools and classes can now be challenged to rise to the standards set and achieved by such homes. I would like to see the nursery area of schooling officially invested with the major task of getting the pupils ready for reading. If, by age five, the majority of children were so ready, it would be possible to answer the question 'Who does what?' by more closely defining responsibility for teaching the following broad stages:

Stage 1   The nursery school
Prereading. A programme of carefully graded experiences based on chapters 3–6 of this book.

Stage 2   The reception class
Term 1   Teaching the letters – this to include visual recognition, correct sounding, and ability to write all capital and lower case forms.
Terms 2 and 3   Starting the reading scheme or approach, and continuing the phonic work systematically through simple blending.

Stage 3   Middle and upper infant classes
Developing independence by completing the reading scheme and continuing systematic phonic work through more difficult blends and letter strings to the syllabification of long words.

Stage 4   Junior and secondary schools
Extending the already competent reader in the areas of critical and efficient reading and promoting the reading habit. (I have suggested a number of ways in which these aims may be achieved in *Reading Development and Extension* [Walker 1974].)

Without a more committed reading drive on the part of schools, beginning reading will continue to occupy a major part of schooling for many children. Such a drive can only be accomplished by heads of schools being prepared to allocate teachers and resources to specific reading tasks. I am sure that teachers would welcome a tighter definition of their roles, particularly in a subject like reading where a teacher depends so much on what has been done (or not done) by the teachers in preceding classes. Also, though I would not wish to question the freedom of schools to do what they think best for their children, I feel that we can, while retaining freedom, do much more to prepare our pupils for subsequent stages of schooling, so that each teacher and child can build on what has gone before. This implies a progression, in which each area of schooling acknowledges its responsibility for certain goals and sets about achieving them. We have been handicapped in establishing such a progression by the lack of a firm base on which to build. Consequently, our infant schools have been saddled with a multiplicity of reading tasks which have involved almost every infant teacher working at every stage of reading simultaneously. With the expansion of nursery education, the teaching of reading has been given the base on which a successful superstructure can be built. If the nursery school can get its children ready for reading, the infant school can go on from there and establish the basic competence and independence which the junior and secondary schools require for their tasks in reading extension.

Finally, though I would regard prereading as the major concern of the nursery school, I see no reason why the more able and educationally mature children should not begin formal reading while still of preschool age. It is extremely frustrating for the bright four year old, who is in every sense ready, to have to defer the joy of actually reading until he is officially 'old enough' i.e. until he joins the infant school.

References
STOTT, D. H. (1971) *Programmed Reading Kit* Edinburgh: Holmes McDougall

Chapter 8

Recording and guiding progress

Intuitive assessments of readiness

Many teachers claim that they can detect intuitively the magic moment when a child is ready to read, and this without ever putting pen to paper or recording systematically the many indications of readiness. I view such claims with suspicion. In the first place making judgments which may have the most important implications for a child's whole future in such an off the cuff manner reflects a dangerous complacency. Secondly, these claims represent a limited and oversimplified awareness of the vast amount and quality of experience and ability which the child himself needs to bring to make reading possible. Without in any way wishing to shroud prereading in a cloak of overcomplexity, I do feel that in the third quarter of the twentieth century we should approach this important area in an organized way and with greater professionalism. The myth that anyone can teach small children is still not entirely dispelled. Such a view of the teaching role will be perpetuated unless we give greater consideration to the importance of prereading activity for child growth and development. In the first place we should seek to provide essential experience for the development of certain skills which are basic to progress in reading – this is our teaching function. Secondly, we should offer the children opportunities to demonstrate that the skills are already developed – this is our assessment function. It is difficult to see how teaching and assessment can be separated.

The danger of intuitive evaluations of readiness, unsupported by systematic recording, is that readiness may be assumed from too narrow a base of experience. Prereading is synonymous with general maturity. This is an amalgam of maturity in a number of different areas, the most important of which are visual and auditory discrimination, motor and manipulative skills, emotional stability, oral language development and general ability. The latter includes memory, a capacity for sequential thinking, certain powers of imagination and some intelligence. The final stage of prereading is the merging of these different aspects of growth into an ultimate motivation towards books expressed in an irresistible desire on the part of the child to want to read. Accurate assessment of so wide a sampling of experience and behaviour is impossible without detailed teaching, observation and recording.

In my experience, the majority of children in Britain are assessed as ready to read entirely on the basis of teachers' subjective opinions, unsupported by any shred of recorded evidence and frequently without benefit of prereading activities. An even more negative ,approach to assessment is to ignore the need for prereading altogether and to pitch the children into the reading scheme as soon as they have settled in school. Such shock treatment immediately sorts out the sheep from the goats and gives an infallible indication of those who are patently 'not ready'. Unfortunately, the shock of such baptism by books strongly conditions the beginner against all forms of print and all too frequently the victim decides, right at the start, that reading is not for him.

Reading readiness tests

An approach much used in the United States is the out and out testing of reading readiness. However, as American children start school later than do British children the tests have little relevance in Britain. In any case British teachers have an understandable reluctance to subject small children to testing. To have any diagnostic value the tests would have to be administered very early in schooling, certainly during the first term in school. It is obvious that many children at this stage are too immature to make the effort to collaborate with the tester, usually the child's own teacher, and to listen and react to the many directions and oral instructions necessary to generate a sufficient spread of relevant responses. Administrative difficulties preclude the testing of groups of children much exceeding a dozen, even with expert assistance. The tester must constantly ensure that the children are at the right place on the right page; it is easy for the small child, unused to books, to turn over several pages instead of one, while reference to page numbers is valueless as the children are frequently ignorant of number symbols. Care has to be taken to ensure that individuals respond to the practice items in the approved manner. The administrator must also have regard to exact timing and wording of instructions. The need for quiet and freedom from distraction presupposes the presence of an extra room, which in many of our schools is just not available. Even where there is accommodation, average class sizes would necessitate three bouts of testing if all the children were to be involved. In practice, as readiness tests are divided into four or five subareas, each testing one major aspect of prereading, up to fifteen different testing sessions are normally required for the typical class. This does not include additional sessions for those individuals whose difficulties necessitate their being tested on a one to one basis.

Administrative difficulties apart, test results are only valid when the testee gives of his best. This cannot be guaranteed with the small child who, in the first few weeks of school, has already decided that learning is not for him. He reacts to testing with the same strategies which he finds effective in avoiding all learning in school.

Reading readiness profiles

Despite the difficulties inherent in testing, I feel that there is a need in Britain for more objective measures to which teachers can relate their own subjective observations and opinions. This has now become possible with the publication of the *Thackray Reading Readiness Profiles* (1974). These are the first original British readiness tests to be published and are the culmination of a decade of research in the field with British children by Derek and Lucy Thackray. The profiles comprise three group measures:

1 vocabulary and concept development
2 auditory discrimination
3 visual discrimination

The fourth profile provides an individual measure of general ability. This is an adaptation of the Harris revision of the Goodenough Draw-a-Man Test, normed for British children. The profiles give direct measures of the four abilities mentioned. However, in order to complete the profiles the child must attend, follow directions and examine the content in left–right sequence, so that these particular abilities are measured too, albeit indirectly.

The profiles are intended to be set after five or six weeks in school when the children are acclimatized to classroom routines and have acquired some experience in listening and reacting to instructions. In the case of those children whose overt behaviour in a wide-ranging way indicates all round maturity of a high order, I myself would be sorely tempted to shorten the acclimatization period recommended. There is little doubt, as the authors state, that the results will indicate quite clearly those children who are strong in all the reading readiness measures and who could learn to read with success at once. For such children prereading in school is an irrelevance and early testing would obviate the need for activities which could be highly frustrating and undemanding. If one group of children can make a good start on reading very early in school, this is not only a source of great personal satisfaction and achievement to the children concerned, it also provides many of the other children with great motivation towards wanting to read.

Some children are so patently immature in every way that there seems little point in testing them in order to ascertain that they must not be hurried into reading. Where the profiles may be particularly useful is with the majority of children who are neither obviously ready nor unready. In these cases the profiles can be used diagnostically to indicate areas of specific weakness. Such information enables the teacher to concentrate her efforts in the most effective ways and to deal only with those prereading activities and experiences which individual children particularly need. Tests, then, can enable the busy teacher to add objective measures to her own subjective observations, not so much in order to decide *when* particular children are ready for reading, but as a help in forming different ability groups, each of which would have specific programmes of work tailored to the precise needs of the children concerned.

At the present time many nursery and reception class teachers see their major role as one of socialization. If they are to rise above this to a truly professional level in which the main roles are expert assessment, diagnosis and treatment of learning difficulties, they will need to have much smaller classes than they have at present.

Reading readiness records

One of the problems of readiness testing is that for administrative and other reasons, only a limited sampling of experience and aptitude can be measured. Admittedly, the four Thackray profiles deal with areas which most experts in the field agree to be among the most important as indicators. Incidentally they are, of course, the areas which are most easily measured. In the case of emotional factors, only partial assessments can be made and these only by inference about the way in which the children tackle the test items. For this to be done with any thoroughness, testing would have to be done individually. Tests can only measure performance on one given occasion and if a child has an off day or, for some reason, is not cooperative, diagnoses may be made and subsequent treatment prescribed on the basis of inaccurate data.

Many factors important in child growth towards reading are impossible for teachers to control or influence. Others are not susceptible to testing. In order to obtain the widest possible view of the developing child, testing needs to be supplemented by repeated recorded observations of children in numerous learning and experiential situations. Many hundreds of teachers both on preservice and in-service courses have found my reading readiness record (see page 106) helpful not only in recording progress, but also in drawing up a comprehensive programme of prereading activities using traditional materials and approaches. The asterisked items are all obtainable from Philip and Tacey. In the auditory discrimination section, the items labelled 'Hear differences' and 'Look, say and listen' refer to

READING READINESS RECORD
Name

MATCHING AND SORTING
beads ☐   ribbons ☐   buttons ☐
*profile counters ☐   shapes ☐

PATTERN MAKING
*Tripat ☐   *Multipat ☐

jigsaws ☐   Lego ☐   Snap ☐

*DISCRIM APPARATUS
A ☐   B ☐   C ☐   D ☐
3 ☐   4 ☐   5 ☐   6 ☐
7 ☐   8 ☐   9 ☐   10 ☐

*HEREWARD OBSERVATION TEST
A ☐ B ☐ C ☐ D ☐ E ☐ F ☐
G ☐ H ☐ I ☐ J ☐ K ☐ L ☐

*ALIKE AND UNALIKE STRIP BOOKS
A ☐ B ☐ C ☐ D ☐ E ☐ F ☐ G ☐ H ☐

CONVERSATION
with peers ☐   with teacher ☐

MEMORY SPAN
nursery rhymes ☐

SEQUENTIAL THINKING
retelling a story ☐

IMAGINATION
completing a story ☐

AUDITORY DISCRIMINATION
I Spy ☐   Hear differences ☐   Look, say and listen ☐

HAND/EYE COORDINATION
cutting out ☐   colouring ☐   tracing ☐
catching 7" ball ☐   Plasticine ☐

EMOTIONAL DEVELOPMENT
confidence ☐   effort ☐   participation ☐

GENERAL MATURITY ☐

GENERAL INTELLIGENCE
Goodenough Test score ☐   mental age ☐

activities featured in *Getting Ready for Reading*, Books 1 and 2. In the boxes alongside each item the teacher assesses the child's level of competence on a five-point scale from A to E. The first three sections on the record remind the teacher to start at concrete level. The next three sections suggest work with graded material, in visual discrimination. The only objective measure included in the record is the Goodenough Draw-a-Man Test. This is intended as a final check against which the teacher can evaluate her own observations of general development. In my experience, the more mental age exceeds 6·5, the greater the success in early reading.

The record is a constant reminder to teachers of the great width of activity involved in prereading and provides implicit warnings not to rush children into print. It is a help in forming ability groups. The more mature children forge ahead rapidly through the activities. The slower ones are easily identified and can be given extra help. When children move into higher classes before the prereading activity is completed the record can save much duplication and overlapping. The new teacher merely needs to consult the record and start the child 'where he is'. Inadequate recording frequently results in the omission of important experiences. Teachers assume that new children coming into their classes may have done things which have in fact not been done at all. Recording and good communication between class teachers should ensure that nothing important has been missed when children change teachers.

Recording by structured materials

The readiness record referred to above constantly reminds the teacher of the need to diversify the activities associated with prereading. Without by any means forming a straitjacket which will stifle teacher initiative, it does make suggestions as to the sort of materials which seem to be helpful in promoting certain kinds of activity. In other instances, e.g. conversation, it is quite open-ended and leaves the teacher free to use her ideas of how particular areas might be assessed. However, in the case of inexperienced teachers or those who lack specific training for the task, open-ended approaches in prereading are of little value.

Opportunities to record are of no use if the teacher does not know what is worth recording, and how this may best be done. The best form of recording is testing work which has been well taught. Here we test not only the relevance of our own teaching but the responses of the children to what we teach. If our teaching is inadequate or of poor quality, whatever we record will not help children very much. Nor will they be helped if we teach the wrong things or miss important things out. What large numbers of teachers seem to need above all is a good solid programme of work on which they can base their teaching. It needs to be structured in a good progression of gradually increasing difficulty and be sufficiently varied to ensure that the most important aspects of prereading are taught well. There are numerous materials about but they are very diverse and come from a number of different sources. Many teachers lack the confidence and expertise to organize these into an orderly working scheme. Given a set of materials, the validity of which they accept, most teachers would prefer a package, supported by a good manual. The children would go through the items in the kit at their own best rate and the teacher would simply record them at work. Such a kit would give the untrained and inexperienced teacher something to build on and should be versatile enough to give opportunities for whole class or large group teaching and for working with small groups or individuals as well.

Though kits and packages abound in junior schools and beyond, there is hardly anything that is really useful for the teacher of prereaders. It may be that the would-be designers are familiar with the severe financial stringency under which our infant/nursery schools are accustomed to working. Nursery/infant teachers also, in the past, have had a 'do it yourself' attitude towards the design and manufacture of materials which has amounted to an occupational disease. However, I have detected increasing dissatisfaction with inadequate materials and with the constant need to go on churning out work cards and the like for long hours in so-called 'free time'.

Flying Start
A recent innovation which many teachers of preschool and reception class children are finding helpful is the *Flying Start Kit*, developed by D. H. Stott and published in this country by Holmes McDougall. The theory behind the materials is that before the child can learn to read or do anything else in school, he must first learn how to learn. Though not designed specifically as a prereading kit, *Flying Start* has many ingredients which are invaluable as the very earliest stages in a prereading programme. There are four sets of picture puzzles, divided respectively into two, four, six and eight pieces. The six and eight piece puzzles are animal pictures. In addition, there are two sets of 'What's happening' pictures, one of four pieces, the other of five. In these puzzles the child is encouraged to discover the logic of what is happening in each picture and to verbalize his findings to the teacher. In all these activities, trial and error methods are discouraged and the child is trained to attack the puzzles in a systematic way. As there are no colours, shape or link cues to help him the child must attend to the meaning.

The 'Merry-go-rounds' are puzzles in four different stages, each consisting of eight pieces. The pieces are fitted together to make a circle.

Four of the pieces have stars and four have dots. The children take turns in pairs to fit the pieces but as one child has all the stars and his partner has all the dots, each has to learn to be patient and to await his turn.

Matching is done in two ways, first using lower case letters in a traditional posting activity known as 'Mail boxes'. There are three sets of mail boxes with three letters to each, giving a choice of nine letters. Each set is colour coded. The pink set is the easiest, followed by the yellow. In the final, blue set the confusingly similar letters b, d, p and q have to be matched. The other discriminatory tasks are set through the 'Matchers'. These consist of twelve sets of cards, graded into three groups of four and colour-coded as for the mail boxes. There are two types of difference to be noted as well as left–right distinction. If the child chooses two correctly matched cards the bars on their backs correspond.

There is an excellent manual which has many practical suggestions for using the materials in the most interesting and effective ways. Record cards are available, which help the teacher not only to plot progress through the kit but also to make useful assessments of the quality of the learning styles being developed.

All the activities are very easy. The game structure heightens motivation. The child is never asked to take too great a step at any one stage. He starts with confidence, is rewarded by success and thus is encouraged to undertake more demanding tasks in a gradual order of increasing difficulty. I regard the prime purpose of the kit as to encourage the child who lacks confidence to begin to try.

Flying Start appears to me to have a number of very useful applications. It seems to be ready-made for the nursery class and preschool playgroup as an essential bridge between the egocentric and unstructured play of early childhood and the more purposeful, cooperative type of learning activity associated with starting school. In disadvantaged areas it would provide essential early experiences for the majority of school beginners. Indeed, it seems to be ideal material for almost all children in the first few weeks of school. This is a time when none of the children can read or write or occupy themselves for longer than a few moments without the teacher's constant support. The more activities the teacher has to hand at this particularly difficult settling-in period, the more the teacher can satisfy diverse needs and ease the way to adjustment. At this time, the teacher could expect the very bright children to go rapidly through the materials. Thus they can act as a screening device which helps to identify the high fliers without recourse to formal testing. Such early identifications enable the teacher to organize more challenging activities for these children to prevent boredom, frustration and possibly disruptive behaviour. Children who by their reactions to the activities reveal the need for a slower programme can go through the kit at a more leisurely pace. In almost every class in the infant school there is a nucleus of children who invariably find all they are asked to do beyond them. Even the simplest task is too hard. It may be that the tasks we set really are too hard and that we do not simplify them enough. If I had only one such child I would buy *Flying Start* for him. What a blessed relief to the child himself, to the other children who are too frequently the victims of his distractibility, and to his teacher, when at last here is something which he can do. Once a child begins to make some positive effort, to show the tiniest spark, then hope kindles within us. We know the child need not fail.

The Prereading Workshop

The *Prereading Workshop*, which is to be published in three stages by Ward Lock Educational, is based on the main ideas in this book. It aims to present at reasonable cost a complete package of prereading materials. Some of the apparatus is large enough to be used for whole-class, or if preferred, large-group teaching. Almost all the teacher's apparatus is duplicated on a small scale so that the children can practise with it and thus reinforce the concepts taught directly. There is a detailed manual which explains the rationale of the *Workshop* and gives full suggestions for using it.

The Prereading Workshop Stage 1

Stage 1 of the *Prereading Workshop* was published in April 1976. The programme starts with the *Look, Listen and Tell* pictures. These are large posters which can be seen by an entire class if the children are suitably seated. They are, of course, equally suitable for small-group work as well. The four brightly coloured pictures depict respectively home, street, farm and seaside scenes. Accompanying the pictures is a tape cassette in four sections, two each side. The sections reproduce respectively sounds associated with the objects, persons and creatures represented in the four large conversation pictures. The pictures and cassette give the teacher great scope to develop vocabulary and oral language concepts as well as visual and auditory discrimination either with the whole class or with selected groups.

The second item consists of the giant *Going Shopping* pictures. These four posters, which are the same size as the *Look, Listen and Tell* pictures, portray a toy shop, a greengrocer's, a supermarket and an outfitter's. The children are encouraged to name and discuss the objects displayed in the different shops. As with the *Look, Listen and Tell* pictures, the manual gives detailed suggestions for developing concepts of shape, size, colour, texture, position, number and function. Auditory work is extended and there are suggestions for social training and practical, dramatic and constructional activities.

Concepts introduced in the above activities are practised and consolidated in the *Going Shopping* matching game. For this activity the four large shop posters should be hung at convenient points about the classroom and a child assigned to each as 'shopkeeper'. Each shopkeeper has a *checking card* on one half of which is a small-scale replica of his shop and on the other a section divided into six squares, on each of which is printed a picture representing an object in that shop, so that there are six pictures to each card.

The *matching cards* are shuffled and drawn by four children who, when all the cards are dealt, should have six each. Children must first decide to which shop each card should be taken. The task is more difficult than normal matching activity for, although the drawings on the matching cards correspond exactly with those on the checking cards, they are drawn in one colour only and are not brightly coloured like the objects in the *Going Shopping* pictures. To make the task more difficult still, some of the objects are viewed from different angles than those in the *Going Shopping* pictures. This is designed to:

1 make the children attend closely to the task
2 give practice in orientation

When a player thinks he has accurately related a matching card to a certain shop he presents it to the appropriate shopkeeper. The latter then checks the matching card against his own checking card. If there is a perfect match he accepts the card. If there is no match he gives the card back and the player must try another shop.

Alternatively the giant pictures may be dispensed with and four children may each take a checking card and its six related matching cards for individual matching activity.

With the large pictures used so far, the accent will have been on nouns (naming objects and sounds associated with them) and on adjectives developing concepts of shape, size, number, texture, colour, position and function. In the four *Having Fun* pictures the accent is on *doing* (verbs). The posters portray respectively park, school playground, Bonfire Night and Christmas, and lend themselves readily to support topic work if used seasonally at appropriate times.

The *Having Fun* pictures should be of great help in the continuation of oral language development. There is considerable scope for encouraging the children, by appropriate questioning and suggestion, to make inferences about likely causes and results of actions portrayed and to project themselves imaginatively into many of the situations through mime and other dramatic activity.

The *Having Fun* matching games are organized on the same lines as the matching material associated with the *Going Shopping* activities. There are four checking cards, each of which shows a small-scale replica of one of the posters, together with a section of six pictures, each of which shows a different activity from the giant picture. There are twenty-four separate matching cards, divided into four sets of six cards each. They may be used in conjunction with the *Having Fun* pictures for group activity or 'with the checking cards only for individual practice in matching.

Throughout Stage 1 of the *Prereading Workshop* the children are encouraged to develop ideas not directly presented in the pictures, to make inferences, and to use their imagination. The materials are designed to make children think and to verbalize their thinking.

The Prereading Workshop Stage 2
Stage 2 will provide carefully-graded material for teaching fifteen popular nursery rhymes. With the help of a comprehensive manual teachers will be able to develop oral language through repetition, rhythm and rhyme. The material is further aimed to give training in left to right eye movements, visual and auditory discrimination, memory training and sequential thinking. Work in all these areas is reinforced with giant teaching pictures. This may then be consolidated by the children themselves using miniature versions of the giant pictures.

The first items in the Stage 2 programme are the giant *Nursery Rhyme* two-piece pictures. These portray with coloured drawings on white card the following nursery rhymes:

1 Little Miss Muffet
2 Old Mother Hubbard
3 Pussycat, Pussycat
4 Little Bo Peep
5 Georgie Porgie

Each rhyme is presented in two sequences. The pictures should be a real help for teaching the nursery rhymes in sequence. The cards are big enough for teaching a whole class at once though, of course, they can be used with smaller groups if teachers so desire. The pictures make ideal frieze material and few teachers will resist the temptation to caption them suitably and thus introduce the children to print, possibly for the very first time, in a meaningful way. The children are then given extra practice with the small two-piece pictures. As they play individually or in pairs they should be encouraged to tell what is happening in each picture until they have mastered these nursery rhymes with enjoyment and understanding.

The giant *Nursery Rhyme* three-piece pictures extend the work already done in the two-piece pictures to left to right eye movements involving three horizontal fixations. The rhymes in this section are:

1   Humpty Dumpty
2   Come, let's to Bed
3   Little Boy Blue
4   Ladybird, Ladybird
5   Wee Willie Winkie

The children then practise individually with the miniature versions of the three-piece *Nursery Rhyme* pictures. There are link cues to assist correct sequencing. Incidentally the designers have really exerted themselves to eliminate from the illustrations the archaic overfussiness traditionally associated with nursery-rhyme pictures and to invest the characters and situations with a timeless yet lively and direct quality.

The giant four-piece *Nursery Rhyme* pictures help to teach the following rhymes:

1   Goosy, Goosy, Gander
2   Hey Diddle Diddle
3   The Lion and the Unicorn
4   There was a Crooked Man
5   Jack and Jill

Linking cues make it possible to arrange the sequences in the following pattern:

1   2
3   4

and thus to practise complete eye movements of the kind involved in connected reading i.e. two left to right horizontal fixations followed by a backward and downward sweep to the start of the next line below. This extension of eye training is additional to the general language work, visual and auditory discrimination, sequencing, memory training, frieze-making and captioning to which the nursery rhyme pictures lend themselves so readily. The work is consolidated by the children themselves using their own smaller versions of the pictures.

The *Three Bears* giant pictures enable the teacher to build up this favourite story with the children in groups both large and small. There is tremendous scope for questioning, discussion, anticipation and imagination as the story unfolds, as well as for sequential thinking, memory training, re-telling, frieze-making and captioning. When the story has been well taught the children can reconstruct it for themselves with the eleven miniature versions of the giant pictures.

The Prereading Workshop Stage 3
Stage 3 provides carefully graded material which, supported by a detailed manual, will help children to recognize the letter-shapes (both capital and lower case), to write them and to learn their correct phonic sounds.

The Stage 3 programme starts with the *Capital Letter Matching Cards* and boxes which introduce the children to their first experience of matching abstract symbols (experience of matching at concrete level is presupposed before this activity is undertaken). There are four letter boxes, one for each of the following groups of letters:

1 ABDE
2 FGHI
3 JKLM
4 NQRT

There are sixteen cards, one for each of the above letters. This is a non-directed, self-correcting, posting activity which trains the children to look closely and observe differences. The children play in pairs or groups of five—four checking, one posting. The sixteen capital letters in this section are those whose form differs from that of their lower-case counterparts. As the capital are more distinctive than lower-case forms, this is an easy matching activity, providing the children look closely and attend to what they are doing. No attempt is made at this stage to teach the sounds associated with these symbols.

The *Yellow Post Office* introduces the lower-case counterparts of the sixteen capital letters already met. Four post offices and sixteen cards provide self-correcting matching practice for children either working in pairs or in groups of five. Still there is no attempt at teaching sounds.

In the *Green Post Office* the children meet the ten letters whose capital and lower-case forms are identical. Three boxes are assembled, one for each of the following letter groups:

1 COP
2 UVS
3 WXYZ

There are ten cards, one for each of the above letters. This is a self-correcting, letter-matching activity at which the children play either in pairs or in groups of four (three checking, one posting). As with the previous letter-matching exercises, there is at this stage no attempt to attach a sound value to the symbols. The children are being introduced gradually to shapes which they will soon be meeting in words and sentences. The shapes are used here to train them to attend to what they are doing and to look closely.

In the *Red Post Office* practice is given in matching the pairs of letters whose upper and lower-case forms are different. Letter boxes are assembled to receive letter groups as follows:

1 Aa Bb Dd Ee
2 Ff Gg Hh Ii
3 Jj Kk Ll Mm
5 Nn Qq Rr Tt

There are sixteen cards, one for each of the letter pairs. The symbols have all been met in previous exercises though not in juxtaposition. Still the accent is on close attention and visual discrimination. No sound values are related to the symbols in pairs.

With the first set of *Giant Letter Sounding Cards* the teacher introduces two important aspects of learning. She teaches the correct phonic sounds of the letters. As the child learns these he also learns to write them. Both capital and lower-case letters are introduced at the same time. The cards are designed to enable the teacher to teach the correct phonic sounds of all the letters of the alphabet (except the letter x). The cards have many subsidiary uses, e.g. as alphabet friezes, handwriting models and 'I Spy' stimuli. As each group of five letters is mastered the children practise the newly learned sounds with their own smaller versions of the letter-sounding cards. This self-correcting activity is played in pairs or in small groups, with one child who may be a little ahead of the rest acting as leader. A second set of small cards reinforces the work.

A set of twenty-five 'I Spy' cards provides further extension and reinforcement of the phonic work. Children play at this activity in pairs or small groups. The final item in the kit is the comprehensive teachers' manual.

It is hoped that by using the *Prereading Workshop* the need for special diagnostic testing will be eliminated and that children will be prevented from being needlessly hurried into print before they are ready. The fact that they know all their letter sounds and can write the letters as well should be of great help to them whatever method of formally beginning reading is adopted. Finally the materials, designed to develop the subskills leading to reading by providing essential experience for the majority, can also be used in the case of certain children to demonstrate that the skills are already developed and that these children should begin to read at once with confidence and success.

Bibliography

BOWLBY, J. (1964) *Child Care and the Growth of Love* Harmondsworth: Penguin

BERNSTEIN, B. (1971) *Class, Codes and Control* London: Routledge and Kegan Paul

START, K. B. and WELLS, B. K. (1972) *The Trend of Reading Standards* Slough: NFER

SMYTHE, P. C., STENNETT, R. G., HARDY, M. and WILSON, H. R. (1972) Developmental patterns in elemental reading skills: phoneme discrimination *Alberta Journal of Educational Research* 18

SHIACH, G. (1972) *Teach Them to Speak* London: Ward Lock Educational

THACKRAY, D. and L. (1974) *Thackray Reading Readiness Profiles* London: University of London Press

WALKER, C. (1974) *Reading Development and Extension* London: Ward Lock Educational

Index